Memories
of
Southampton

Part of the

Memories

series

*The Publishers would like to thank the following companies for supporting
the production of this book*

Main Sponsor

Southampton City College

Andrews (Shipside Services) Limited

F A Hendy & Lennox (Holdings) Limited

F Musson & Son Limited

Portswood House Limited

Sibley Material Movements Ltd

AR Veal Limited

Warner-Lambert (UK) Limited

Wessex Institute of Technology

First published in Great Britain by True North Books Limited
Units 3 - 5 Heathfield Industrial Park
Elland West Yorkshire
HX5 9AE
Tel. 01422 377977
© Copyright: True North Books Limited 1999

ISBN 1 900463 34 2

Text, design and origination by True North Books Limited
Printed and bound by The Amadeus Press Limited

Memories are made of this

Memories. We all have them; some good, some bad, but our memories of the town we grew up in are usually tucked away in a very special place in our minds. The best are usually connected with our childhood and youth, when we longed to be grown up and paid no attention to adults who told us to enjoy being young, as these were the best years of our lives. We look back now and realise that they were right.

So many memories - perhaps of the war and rationing, perhaps of parades, celebrations and royal visits. And so many changes; one-way traffic systems and pedestrianisation. New trends in shopping that led to the very first self-serve stores being opened.

Through the bad times and the good, however, Southampton not only survived but prospered. We have only to look at the city as it is today, to see what progress has been realised and what achievements have been made over the last 50 years. Southampton has a history to be proud of - but more importantly, a great future to look forward to, into the new millennium and beyond.

Contents

Around the city centre

A moment in time is captured along Above Bar in the 1920s, and a wealth of fascinating detail is preserved for us about a world that has now vanished. For one thing, that wonderful richness and variety of architecture that once greeted the eye is gone. The Sussex Hotel, at far left, provides one good example, whilst directly across the street stands the famous Alexandra Picture Theatre. As the Philharmonic Hall, this building was the first place in Southampton to show moving pictures, back in 1897. Reopened as the Alexandra in 1911, after much refurbishment, it modestly claimed to be undoubtedly the finest Picture Theatre in this Country. It did good business, and was only closed and demolished in 1933 to make way for a bigger cinema, The Regal. However, in a photograph that is rich in nostalgia, perhaps pride of place goes to the two magnificent open-top trams bound for the Royal Pier and Swaythling. They had to be lower than normal trams to get through the arch of Bargate safely. Also the picture shows another supposed safety measure, by which upper-deck passengers avoided decapitation by sitting on back-to-back knifeboard seats which ran lengthways down the middle of the tram.

Events of the 1930s

HOT OFF THE PRESS

The years of the 1930s saw Adolf Hitler's sickening anti-Jewish campaign echoed in the streets of Britain. On 19th October 1936 Oswald Mosley's 7,000-strong British Union of Fascists clashed head on with thousands of Jews and Communists in London, resulting in 80 people being injured in the ensuing battle. Mosley and his 'blackshirts' later rampaged through the streets beating up Jews and smashing the windows of their businesses.

GETTING AROUND

At the beginning of the decade many believed that the airship was the transport of the future. The R101 airship, however, loaded with thousands of cubic metres of hydrogen, crashed in France on its maiden flight in 1930. Forty-eight passengers and crew lost their lives. In 1937 the Hindenburg burst into flames - the entire disaster caught on camera and described by a distraught reporter. The days of the airship were numbered.

SPORTING CHANCE

In 1939 British racing driver Sir Malcolm Campbell hit the headlines when he captured the world's water-speed record for the third time in 'Bluebird' - all his cars were given the same name. A racing driver who set world speed records both on land and on water, Sir Malcolm established world land-speed records no fewer than nine times. His son Donald went on to set further records, tragically dying in 1967 when his speedboat - also named 'Bluebird' - crashed.

This view of High Street looking towards Bargate is one to linger over and savour, particularly as so much that is there is no longer with us. That ancient survivor, the Bargate itself, is an honourable exception. The date of this inter-wars shot is unspecified, although film buffs might be able to pin it down from the programme advertised at the Gaiety - Chester Morris in *The Infernal Machine* and George O'Brien in *Smoke Lightning*. The Gaiety is no longer to be seen, nor is the

superb classical frontage of All Saints Church, to the right. Gone from the streets too are the scarlet and white trams, with their distinctive deep domed roofs known as Bargate design. The medieval arch of Bargate had presented a persistent challenge to the trams of Southampton. Even the earlier open-tops had been lower than normal, with back-to-back knifeboard seating running lengthways down the middle of the upper deck. The low domed roofs of the latter covered trams enabled these too to negotiate the arch until Bargate was by-passed altogether in 1938. Southampton's first trams had been horse-drawn vehicles, back in 1879. The Corporation took over in 1898 and electrified the system. Trams departed the streets of Southampton in 1949.

Above: Shirley Road offers a fairly tranquil scene in terms of traffic, at least in comparison to its present role as the A3057. The approaching motor-cyclist gives the impression that his speed is a sedate one, and no doubt due care had to be taken with tramlines about. The presence of the trams dates the photograph at pre-1949 (the last year of tram services in Southampton), probably within 10 years of that date. The most striking feature on the picture is St Boniface Church whose tower dominates the skyline. As churches go it is of fairly recent origin, having been built by Jenkins and Sons of Southampton, and opening in 1927. However, it was built in very traditional style. The architecture is Romanesque, and an aerial view would reveal the shape of a Latin cross. The church has impressive features, both inside and outside, and the tone is set by the imposing western frontage, with its massive main entrance doors of Austrian oak. A service from St Boniface was broadcast on the Community Hymn Singing programme, on BBC Radio, in June 1953. The theme of the service was a very appropriate one - a sea-connected community.

Above right: The bottom end of The Avenue, with Asylum Green to the left, provides a pleasant prospect in a shot which seems to suggest a slower pace of life, before the age of mass car ownership. A cyclist makes leisurely progress towards one of Southampton's distinctly domed trams, the presence of which makes the photograph of pre-1949 vintage. The growth of Southampton's reputation as a spa town in the mid-

eighteenth century created a need to enhance the approaches to the town. The Avenue (better known to motorists as the A33) was created with its double row of elms, later to be replaced by chestnuts, limes and maples. Asylum Green has a strong historical connection if the word *asylum* is taken to mean *a place of shelter or refuge*. In 1816 a branch of the Royal Military Asylum of Chelsea was set up in this spot. It housed 400 boys, soldiers' sons who had lost one or both parents. The boys were well cared for, although they were awoken early by the beat of a drum, and subject to fairly strict discipline. Boys were replaced by girls in 1823, but by 1840 they had all returned to Chelsea. The Asylum buildings were taken over by the Ordnance Survey Department in 1841.

Memories of **SOUTHAMPTON**

Below: The corner of Bargate Street with Above Bar displays the first tentative efforts at reconstruction in this photograph taken around 1951. New shop frontages are cautiously taking shape, but evidence of the terrible damage done by enemy aircraft is still plain to see. Much of the destruction took place on the night of December 1st 1940, and one local resident wrote vividly of how he awoke the following day to have an uninterrupted view as far as the River Test - a view that had previously been blocked by a mass of buildings bordering Above Bar and clustering around Terminus Station. A few memories might be stirred by the names of the shops on this corner - Winter and Worth, Drages, E Mays (house furnishing) and True Form (shoes). Between True Form and Murdoch's musical instrument shop was the Tivoli public house. Bargate itself is just visible to the far left, and it miraculously

survived the bombing. Perhaps the two rampant lions really did act as guardians of Bargate. Trams had just disappeared from Southampton's streets by this time, but the track of the lines shows how the Corporation had finally solved the problem of Bargate - by going round it.

Bottom: Cinema going was enormously popular in the inter-war years, so much so that two cinemas could exist side-by-side at Above Bar. These were the Picture House and the Classic, as demonstrated by this 1930s photograph. Before the television age brought the world into our sitting rooms, the silver screen was the medium of escape from the routine of everyday life into a world of romance and adventure. The Picture House was the *Rolls Royce* of Southampton cinemas, opening in 1920 with seating for 1600. It also boasted a café and a roof tea garden. During the 1920s it featured all the big silent films accompanied by a resident orchestra. Talkies were introduced in 1929. The Classic was relatively late on the scene, opening up as the Cinenews in 1937, with a 458 seat auditorium. It was renamed the Classic in 1938 - with free milk shakes in the café in honour of the occasion! The real world provided drama enough when German bombs crashed down in November 1940. Both cinemas had to be hastily evacuated. The Picture House was irreparably damaged, and never opened again. The Classic, perhaps because of its smallness, was less badly hit and it survived until 1978.

Above: The striking Tudor House in St Michael's Square makes a magnificent setting for a museum. Its imposing structure seems to dwarf the surrounding property into insignificance, and it provides a physical link with Southampton's rich heritage. It was built in the very early years of the sixteenth century, on the site of earlier medieval houses (some features of which were incorporated into the 16th century building) by Sir John Dawtry, a well-to-do citizen who was the controller of customs and organiser of the town's defences. Through Dawtry's widow the property passed into the hands of the man she now married, Sir Richard Lyster, the wealthiest man in Southampton. Over the next three centuries Tudor House changed hands several times, fortunately retaining its essential Tudor characteristics. However, the existence of the house as we see it today owes itself very much to the public-spiritedness of William Spranger. Purchasing Tudor House, and the associated Norman House, for the sum of £1,450 in 1886, Spranger restored them at considerable personal expense and sold them cheaply to Southampton Corporation in 1911. Tudor House was opened as a Hampshire Museum in 1912. The photograph appears to date from a time quite close to when the building had its last major restoration - the 1930s. The work was sensitively done, even reverting to the traditional method of incorporating animal hair into the plastering.

Below: The ominous gaps on the left-hand side of High Street suggest that this is a post-war shot, but from not long after World War II. The types of vehicles on view seem to confirm this. Bargate can be seen in the distance, Southampton's most famous medieval monument having survived the bombing. Fortunately, so did one or two other fine looking buildings in this section of High Street. Woolwich House, to the far right, has a certain amount of style. So too has the Dolphin Hotel, next to it, although of a very different kind. Indeed the exterior of this public house still remains pretty much the same today. The Dolphin boasts a long history, and it has been suggested that one of its more celebrated visitors was Jane Austen, during her stay in Southampton between 1807 and 1809. The photograph was taken from around the site of the Holy Rood Church, one of the casualties of the blitz of November 30th to December 1st 1940. Known as the Church of the Sailors, a religious foundation had stood on this spot since 1320. The shell of Holy Rood remains today as a memorial to merchant seamen, containing a huge anchor and a tribute to the crew of the Titanic.

The skyline and frontages of East Street hold all that variety of style that made it such an interesting street to stroll along before the second world war. The same could have been said of other streets in the town centre which evolved slowly, creating a richness of diversity as they did so. On the photograph, for example, the clean-cut simplicity of architecture to the far left meets an immediate contrast in the more ornate frontage and gable of the Newcastle Private Bank. The bay window of Carters follows next. Not to be outdone, Lockwood & Bradley boasts some nice ornamentation on top. It seems incredible to think that one massive attack in 1940 could wipe out the work of generations, literally overnight. The most celebrated casualty in the picture was All Saints Church, whose dome towers over the other buildings. All Saints had been built between 1792 and 1795 on the site of a medieval church. This side view does not do justice to its magnificent classical features, which were best seen from High Street. The dome was surmounted by a gold pineapple and weather vane. Jane Austen was a regular worshipper at All Saints during her stay at Castle Square in 1807.

Left: A variety of transport presents itself outside Dock House to the left, and the offices of United States Lines to the right. This photograph is dated September 1960, at the very dawn of the swinging sixties, and scooters were to become beloved of the mods of that era. If any car were to symbolise that time, it would more likely be the Mini rather than anything to be seen here. The administration of the docks was carried out at Dock House from 1872 until 1962. It is a no nonsense building of great simplicity, lacking the elaboration of much Victorian architecture, and plain even by the standards of its neighbour. The name of Canute Chambers may just be seen over the door of the United States Line building, fronting onto Canute Road. Perhaps one of the more stirring sights and sounds for those who worked in Dock House was the arrival of the steam-hauled boat trains. They ran right into the docks to platforms attached to the marine passenger terminals. The boat trains passed Terminus Station to cross Canute Road by Dock House. In 1962 a new Dock Office was opened, and for a time the old Dock House was used by Townsend Thoreson Car Ferries.

Below: The enduring structure of Bargate, with its shields and crenellations, offers a sharp contrast to a blander style of design in this 1960s shot of Above Bar. Whilst Bargate, the ancient northern entrance to the medieval walled town of Southampton had survived the bombing, and even acted as an air raid shelter, much of Above Bar had not. Post-war rebuilding produced a rather monotonous uniformity of style, as evidenced by the frontages to the left of the photograph, but at least Southampton could plead that rebuilding had been forced on them by Hitler. Other towns and cities, less hit by the war, tended to wreak their own destruction on fine buildings in the name of development. Nevertheless the 1960s was a time of increasing prosperity when the shadows of the war were finally dispelled. Above Bar presents a cheerful and bustling scene, and the number of vehicles on the street is proof that the age of the car really had arrived. What was modern in the 1960s, of course, might induce a sigh of nostalgia now. Some readers might recognise the car model in which they made their first hiccoughing attempts at driving - that Morris Traveller perhaps, or that Ford Anglia.

At leisure

Simple summer pleasures as the youngsters splash about in the spacious paddling pool. A few adults dip their toes in too, with the excuse of keeping an eye on the young ones. As urbanisation grew apace in the 19th century, our Victorian forebears knew full well the importance of green spaces as lungs for smoky cities, and Southampton is well blessed in this respect. The Central Parks in the heart of the city are supplemented by the huge 326 acres of Southampton Common in which the featured paddling pool is to be found. The photograph was taken around 1965, and the pool was originally a reservoir, being converted between 1934

> *Acts of 1844 and 1865 made the Common into a public parks area*

and 1937. The records of Southampton householders having grazing rights on the Common date back to 1228, and the town's most ancient law court, the *Court Leet,* held its proceedings each year on a mound at the northern end, by Burgess Road. The town gallows was to be found on the Common, the last hanging there being that of a burglar, in 1785. Acts of 1844 and 1865 made the Common into a public parks area, a huge green space that in its time has hosted horseracing, fairs, agricultural shows and military camps - not forgetting the modern Balloon and Flower Festival.

A world of nostalgia lies in this shot of the Gaiety Picture Theatre, not only because it no longer exists, but also because of the evocative sight of grandly uniformed commissionaires manning the entrance. The names too strike a chord from the past - Bebe Daniels, Ben Lyon, Charles Bickford. Which female could have resisted the urge to see that great heart-throb, Douglas Fairbanks, in *Caesar?* Many cinemas dating from the earlier years of the 20th century began their lives as music halls or theatres, as was the case with the Empire. The Gaiety, however, was built specifically as a cinema on the site of a former grocers, Lipton Ltd of 169 High Street. It opened in 1914, its first film being a patriotic drama, *Loss of the Birkenhead.* The Gaiety seated 800, and boasted a full orchestra to accompany its silent films. It became, however, the first talkie cinema in Southampton with the showing of Al Jolson's *The Singing Fool* in 1929. The fact that the photograph shows the Gaiety proudly advertising Talkies suggests that it dates from the early 1930s. The celebrated semi-Moorish style of the Gaiety's frontage can be seen, although this was much modified in 1939. The Gaiety was closed in 1956.

Events & occasions

Below: The great Trans-Atlantic liners carried many distinguished passengers in their heyday between the wars, and few faces were more familiar to the public in 1923 than that of the Prime Minister, David Lloyd George. He is pictured here on board the Mauretania, in September 1923, accompanied by his wife, Margaret. He was a man of rare charisma, and usually managed to adopt a jaunty air for the camera. In fact the press made much of the revival of his health and appearance after the difficult days of World War I, and the huge responsibilities carried by him at the peace making process at Versailles. The sprig of white heather in Lloyd George's lapel may have been intended to bring him good luck, for he was about to depart for the USA where, no doubt, tricky negotiations lay ahead concerning Britain's war debts to that country. Southampton had already awarded Lloyd George the Freedom of the Borough, but he was not universally popular. The old Liberal Party believed that he had betrayed its principles in pursuit of power, and any true Southampton Liberal might have felt it very appropriate that the film showing at The Atherley, on Shirley Road, was The Prodigal Son.

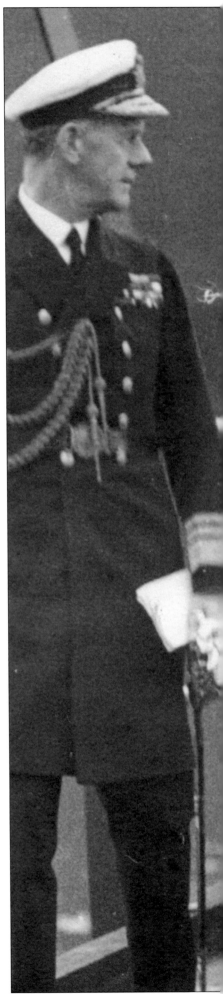

Southampton and its surrounding area has always been a popular visiting spot for members of the royal family, either in an official capacity or for reasons of leisure. Cowes Week was a great attraction, and no doubt visits to Osborne on the Isle of Wight played their part. The various owners of Southampton Docks seemed anxious to show their patriotism and to foster royal connections. In 1890 Queen Victoria opened the Empress Dock, and the Prince of Wales (later Edward VII) carried out the same function for No 5 Dry Dock in 1895, which was named after him. Later still, in 1933, came the opening of the King George V Dry Dock by the King himself. The familiar face on the photograph is that of the Prince of Wales, the future Edward VIII. The occasion is said to date from the 1920s, and judging from the magnificent uniforms on display, it was a naval one. The Prince would go on to take the throne in 1936, and abdicate the same year because of his refusal to sever his relationship with the American divorcee, Mrs Wallis Simpson. They became the Duke and Duchess of Windsor, and were frequent Cunard passengers in the post-war years. On one occasion 75 suitcases were counted into their suite on the Queen Elizabeth, with 70 more trunks going in the hold!

Events of the 1930s

SCIENCE AND DISCOVERY

By observing the heavens, astronomers had long believed that there in the constellation of Gemini lay a new planet, so far undiscovered. They began to search for the elusive planet, and a special astronomical camera was built for the purpose. The planet Pluto was discovered by amateur astronomer Clyde Tombaugh in 1930, less than a year later.

WHAT'S ON?

In this heyday of the cinema, horrified audiences were left gasping at the sight of Fay Wray in the clutches of the giant ape in the film 'King Kong', released in 1933. Very different but just as gripping was the gutsy 1939 American Civil War romance 'Gone with the Wind'. Gable's parting words, 'Frankly, my dear, I don't give a damn' went down in history. 1936 - Britain set up the world's first television service - black and white, of course. The Queen's coronation in 1953, the first such ceremony to be televised, did much to popularise television.

ROYAL WATCH

The talking point of the early 1930s was the affair of the Prince of Wales, who later became King Edward VIII, and American divorcee Wallis Simpson. Faced with a choice, Edward gave up his throne for 'the woman I love' and spent the remainder of his life in exile. Many supported him, though they might not have been as keen to do so if they had been aware of his Nazi sympathies, kept strictly under wraps at the time.

The new Labour Government which came to power in 1945 felt that it was its duty to build a brave new world, and how these Southampton children needed and deserved it. The immensely popular Aneuran Bevan, a key figure in the government, is pictured here mingling with children during a visit he made to the town around this time. The children of Southampton had been in the front line of danger during World War II, and many had been evacuated into Dorset and North Hampshire in the

first two days of September 1939. With no immediate bombing taking place, a drift back had occurred, so a further evacuation of children took place in June 1940, after the first air attacks on the town. The blitz of late November and early December 1940 brought hundreds of homeless people, children amongst them, arriving at rescue centres. Resources of food, clothing, bedding and medical supplies were stretched to the limit. Many would not stay in Southampton at all, and trekked into the countryside, seeking safety. As Minister of Health, Bevan believed that children deserved a better deal, none more so than those who had endured the hardships of war, and he was the architect of the National Health Service, embodying the principle of free medical care for all.

Main picture: Lady Jellicoe and Sir Harry Haig exchange a little joke in this photograph of May 1942, but the pleasant garden party atmosphere masked a more serious purpose. The occasion took place at Eastleigh when Lady Jellicoe, a national vice-president of the British Legion (women's section), presented the Hampshire British Legion's second mobile canteen to Sir Harry Haig, Commissioner for Civil Defence, Southern Region. The presentation had its poignant side, for the mobile canteen was dedicated to the memory of Mrs Ada West, a dedicated British Legion worker who had been killed by enemy action at Eastleigh in 1940, during the mayoralty of her husband, Alderman S F West. The bouquet of roses held by Lady Jellicoe was presented by Sheila West, the grand-daughter of Mrs West, and in a touching speech Alderman

West said that nothing would have pleased mother more than to know that something dedicated to her would help others. This underlined the real gravity of the occasion, for the mobile canteen was to stand ready to proceed to any blitzed area as part of an emergency feeding operation, and Lady Jellicoe expressed the hope that it would be little used for its primary purpose.

Inset: The Hampshire British Legion Women's Section was to staff both mobile canteens in any emergency, and it was one of many bodies that supported Civil Defence. The presentation ceremony was followed by a parade, and other organisations represented were Air Raid Precaution, Fire Guards, Casualty Services, the Red Cross, Rescue Services, the St John's Ambulance Brigade and the Home

Guard. The photograph shows Sir Harry Haig inspecting local units of the Home Guard, accompanied by Major P Hinness, with in the rear Brigadier-General T N S Howard, Hampshire County President of the British Legion. In the anticipation of massive civilian casualties from bombing, the government had attached prime importance to Civil Defence from the outbreak of war. Whilst most organisations under the umbrella of Civil Defence saw their main purpose as dealing with the effects of bombing, the Home Guard had been created in 1939 specifically to counter an enemy invasion. Set up as the L D V (Local Defence Volunteers) their weapons were often little more than knives, clubs and ancient shotguns. Often composed of men that were too young or too old to fight, guarding strategic points against enemy parachutists, cynics had suggested that L D V ought to stand for `Look, Duck and Vanish.' These smartly turned out men on parade in 1942, with bayonets fixed, had come a long way since those early days.

Events of the 1930s

MELODY MAKERS
Throughout the 1930s a young American trombonist called Glenn Miller was making his mark in the world of music. By 1939 the Glenn Miller sound was a clear leader in the field; his clean-cut, meticulously executed arrangements of numbers such as 'A String of Pearls' and 'Moonlight Serenade' brought him fame across the world as a big-band leader. During a flight to England from Paris in 1944 Miller's plane disappeared; no wreckage was ever found.

THE WORLD AT LARGE
In India, Gandhi's peaceful protests against British rule were gathering momentum. The Salt Laws were a great bone of contention: forced to buy salt from the British government, thousands of protestors marched to the salt works, intending to take it over in the name of the Indian people. Policemen and guards attacked the marchers, but not one of them fought back. Gandhi, who earned for himself the name 'Mahatma' - Great Soul - was assassinated in 1948.

INVENTION AND TECHNOLOGY
With no driving tests or speed restrictions, 120,000 people were killed on the roads in Britain between the two world wars. In 1934 Percy Shaw, invented a safety device destined to become familiar the world over: reflecting roadstuds. In dark or foggy conditions the studs that reflected light from the car's headlights kept traffic on the 'straight and narrow' and must over the years have saved many lives.

The heavy German air attacks on Southampton towards the end of November 1940, during which over 200 were killed and something like 400 seriously injured, had not gone unnoticed. The visit of King George VI, on December 5th 1940, was a recognition of the ordeal suffered by the citizens of Southampton. The photograph shows the King outside the Civic Centre, having the extent of the damage explained to him by local officials with the aid of a plan. The King had laid the foundation stone of the Civic Centre on July 1st 1930, whilst still the Duke of York. It had been completed in 1938, at a cost of £750,000, but by late 1940 had sustained damage estimated at £250,000. The human cost had been high too, and no doubt the King was informed of the terrible tragedy of the School of Art students, who had been killed by a bomb penetrating into the very basement of the Civic Centre a month previously. The royal visitor met various representatives of Civil Defence organisations, and in a quick tour of the town and docks was greeted by cheering crowds. Shortly after the King had left, it was found that he had passed within a few yards of an unexploded bomb wedged deep beneath the Forum Cinema.

Above: The arrival of the Red Funnel tender Calshot at 107 Berth, Southampton Docks, on October 14th 1953, was an occasion of more than usual joy and emotion. The Calshot was packed with 150 ex-prisoners of war from the Korean conflict, and the touching scenes on the quayside were reminiscent of those witnessed when the Asturias had brought home the first batch a month previously. This second batch had been transported into Southampton Water by the Empire Orwell before being transferred to the Calshot for the final leg home. The tender was flying the black and amber flag of the Gloucestershire Regiment, for many of the men were Glorious Glosters who had fought so epically against numerically superior Chinese forces at the Imjin River prior to their capture. First ashore was the commanding officer of the `Glosters,' Lieutenant Colonel James P Carne D S O. The returning heroes were given an official welcome by a reception party which included the Mayor of Southampton, Alderman Mrs V P King J P, and civic heads from neighbouring towns. This was a time for tears and reunions, however, rather than speeches, as the ex-prisoners were greeted by their loved ones. Two of the Southampton men involved were Private Norman Gadd, a National Serviceman from Portswood, and Private Reg Budden of Itchen.

Below: On September 28th 1951 the Institute of Electrical Engineers enjoyed a tour around Southampton Docks. There was much to see that day - the arrival of Pretoria Castle from South Africa, or even the unloading of two 4 - 5 litre motor racing boats from the liner Samaria, which were due to compete in the Duke of York's International Gold Trophy on Lake Windermere. Nevertheless it was likely that the star attraction was still Queen Mary, berthed close behind Hotspur IV. This majestic Cunard White Star liner had only recently returned to its peacetime duties, after spending the war as a troopship. She was fitted out for this purpose in Sydney in 1940, her first trooping voyage, involving 5,000 Australian soldiers. She spent much of the rest of the war on the North Atlantic run, making 28 round trips in all, sometimes carrying 15,000 GI's at a time. Of course the U boats were after both the Queens, with high financial rewards to any captain who sank one, but they were simply too fast. Both luxury and speed were the hallmarks of Queen Mary, and in 1951 she still held the Blue Riband for the fastest Atlantic crossing, achieved in 1938 with a time of 3 days, 20 hours and 40 minutes (31.69 knots).

A group of civic officials pose before one of the great ships of the 20th century. The occasion was in April 1980 and the place was almost certainly the Queen Elizabeth II Terminal. It seemed to many that the rise of air travel had ended the great days of the passenger liners forever. Even so, in the early 1960s several new passenger liners entered service, the most famous of all being the P & O's Canberra. Built by Harland and Wolff at Belfast, and launched in 1961, the Great White Whale weighed 44,807 tons and could carry 2,238 passengers. Once the port facilities at Southampton had been modernised to

handle the ship, this became her terminal. Beginning her career by taking emigrants to Australia, the Canberra soon became the cruise ship *par excellence*, a watchword for luxury. No doubt it was the experience of a lifetime to lounge on the sundecks, take a dip in the swimming pool or have

fun at the Bonita Club. Canberra was taken out of service in 1997, but not before one brief change of role. She was stripped down to be a troopship in the Falklands War of 1982, and in the process astonished observers witnessed the removal of no less than 10 grand pianos!

Wartime

Below centre: 'GAS BOMB FELL HERE.' This notice-board straddling the rails carried a chilling message in February 1943, but luckily it was all part of a Civil Defence exercise. Perhaps greater than the fear of orthodox bombing, the possible consequences of a heavy enemy air attack using gas bombs or other chemical weapons loomed large in the government's planning. One problem was that in spite of newsreels showing the horrific effects of bombing during the Spanish Civil War (1936-9), it had been difficult to make the public take the issue seriously before 1939. Many people preferred to bury their heads in the sand, refusing to contem-plate gas attacks or bombing of any kind. In Southampton, for example, civilian respirators were issued free in 1938, but many went in dustbins or were sold to tourists. Nevertheless, the government carried out numerous exercises before the war aimed at combating gas or chemical attack. Personnel were trained to act as mobile units and decontamination centres were set up.

Below: This picture shows one of these decontamination squads in action in the exercise of February 1943. The men are fully equipped for the job, with the better quality gas masks, specially treated oilskins and rubber gumboots. However, the man on the far right appears to be minus one glove, which was probably against the regulations. Also, special oilskin hoods were available in the event of an attack using liquid blister gas, for in this case every inch of bare skin had to be protected. Decontamination involved boiling the garments if they had been touched by any sort of gas. The war had prepared the people of Southampton to expect the unexpected by 1943, and strange sights had become commonplace. Nevertheless these men must have presented a weird, even frightening sight. The calm background, with the engine gently steaming, was a reminder of the stability of the past. The foreground, a mass of oilskins and helmets, represented the uncertain present. The fact that no gas attacks had come by 1943, and bombing of any sort was sporadic by this date, was no reason to lessen vigilance. There was a theory that once Germany began to lose the war, Hitler would resort to any desperate act, if only out of revenge. The later V1 and V2 attacks were of this nature. Nevertheless no gas attacks ever came. This was not out of the kindness of Hitler's heart, but out of the fear of massive retaliation in kind by the Allies.

A nightmarish vision is presented outside the Air Raid Precaution Depot, in July 1942, featuring creatures looking as if they have stepped out of some science fiction or horror film. These were, in fact, members of the decontamination team of ARP, training dockers in anti-gas techniques. The first essential was the donning of the correct dress - jackets, trousers, hoods and gloves made of specially treated oilskin, along with rubber boots and respirators. The entire outfit was extremely heavy, forcing the wearer to take frequent rests. The fear of a gas attack greatly exercised the minds of British government planners in World War II. Gas masks were distributed to the public at large, with an exhortation to carry them everywhere in their little boxes. Some Sotonians will well remember those gas masks, particularly the Mickey Mouse versions for the young. Detailed instructions were given. An imminent gas attack was to be signalled by the Air Raid Warden's rattle. All contaminated clothing was to be destroyed. Anti-gas ointment could be bought at the chemist's shop and applied to any area of the skin affected by liquid blister gas. Fortunately this nightmare scenario never emerged, for gas bombs did not rain down, although the dangers from ordinary bombs fracturing gas mains still existed.

Events of the 1940s

WHAT'S ON?

In wartime Britain few families were without a wireless set. It was the most popular form of entertainment, and programmes such as ITMA, Music While You Work and Workers' Playtime provided the people with an escape from the harsh realities of bombing raids and ration books. In 1946 the BBC introduced the Light Programme, the Home Service and the Third Programme, which gave audiences a wider choice of listening.

GETTING AROUND

October 1948 saw the production of Britain's first new car designs since before the war. The Morris Minor was destined for fame as one of the most popular family cars, while the four-wheel-drive Land Rover answered the need for a British-made off-road vehicle. The country was deeply in the red, however, because of overseas debts incurred during the war. The post-war export drive that followed meant that British drivers had a long wait for their own new car.

SPORTING CHANCE

American World Heavyweight Boxing Champion Joe Louis, who first took the title back in 1937, ruled the world of boxing during the 1930s and 40s, making a name for himself as unbeatable. Time after time he successfully defended his title against all comers, finally retiring in 1948 after fighting an amazing 25 title bouts throughout his boxing career. Louis died in 1981 at the age of 67.

Out of the 150 high explosive bombs and 5000 incendiaries which fell on Southampton in the early hours of July 8th 1941, the Six Dials area received some heavy hits. The railway bridge at the end of St Mary Street just about survived, but a retaining wall and surrounding property sustained much damage. The photograph shows a large gang of men busy at work clearing the line and shoring timbers are in evidence. A policeman looks on as railway wagons are

filled with rubble. Premises belonging to Kent & Co and Finlay & Co appear to be intact. Perhaps most important of all for men who would be working up a thirst, the Brickwoods public house stands ready for business. If the enemy bombers were seeking industrial or communications targets, then in this case at least one of the bombs found its mark. Railways, stations, marshalling yards and goods yards were often targeted, and in the heavy raid of November 23rd 1940 some damage had been inflicted on the Victorian Southampton Terminus station, situated as it was practically on the docks. Also Southampton Central Station, only recently rebuilt in the stylish Odeon type architecture of the 1930s, was hit. Bombs are no respecters of style or age.

Bottom: Heavy bombing of riverside factories along the line of the Itchen did heavy damage in the areas of Bitterne, and Peartree, Newtown, Bevois, All Saints and Northam in the early hours of September 24th 1940. Factories may have been the target, but residential property took a fearsome battering, as these two photographs show. This one is of Belvidere Terrace - a scene of utter devastation. Little is left of the ground floor belonging to the house on the right other than a door on its frame. Officers seem to be anxiously discussing the prospect of the imminent collapse of the upper storey. The German aircraft released 46 high explosive bombs in this raid, resulting in 42 deaths and serious injuries to 163. Terrible risks were attendant on living in the industrialised and dockside areas of Southampton. Close to Belvidere Terrace were the docks and yards of Thornycroft & Co, a huge concern that was vital to the war effort in terms of ship repairing, shipbuilding and marine engineering. The `Luftwaffe' returned to Northam later in the day on September 24th 1940, and two days later 27 bombs fell on Northam gasworks alone, killing 11 workers.

Right: Rescuers pick among the rubble in this picture, which shows more of the consequences of the September 24th attack. The scene this time is Inner Avenue and what were once fine and substantial houses. A gaping hole has been torn out of the one on the right; the one on the left is in even worse condition. Possibly some of the residents are looking on disconsolately, for there seems to be a very small figure in a tin

hat to the left. If so, this must have seemed like a vision from their worst nightmares, unimaginable a few months earlier in spite of all the dire warnings. And yet Southampton just had to be in the front line of attack, with its docks and industries. After all, the Supermarine Company of Southampton had financed and developed Mitchell's K5054, in other words the Spitfire, which was proving such a thorn in the side of the Luftwaffe. Perhaps it was thought by the latter that the heavy hits it made on the Supermarine factory on September 26th 1940 would eliminate the problem. However, Spitfire production was already being dispersed amongst the local motor engineering industry, and lorries carrying parts of Spitfires around Southampton must have done something to lift the spirits.

Above: From around 12.30am to 3.30am, on July 8th 1941, the centre of Southampton was heavily bombed. The number of high explosive bombs which fell was 150, along with 5000 incendiary bombs. Casualties were suffered and thousands of properties were damaged, some being totally destroyed. The two photographs featured show some of the devastation caused in the Six Dials area. This picture gives an indication of the bewilderment and perhaps helplessness that must have been experienced when a familiar landscape has been shattered. Shock seems to be the expression on the face of the woman pushing the bicycle, whilst in the background people pick their way through the rubble, perhaps trying to maintain the routine of going to work as some sort of stabilising factor in a world gone mad. Others stare

uncomprehendingly at the damage. Some landmarks were, of course, still left. The Edinburgh Hotel in the background, at the corner of St Andrew's Road and St Mary's Road, seems to have emerged relatively unscathed, and still proudly advertises its Brickwoods. A similar story applies to the public house on the corner of St Mary's Street, to the left.

Top: The clearing up operation has commenced on this totally devastated building, another casualty in the Six Dials area of the bombing of July 8th 1941. Above the wreckage, to the right, the advertisement for Gordon's Gin must have seemed to represent another world to the toiling workers, a world of normality before the nightmare began. Others must have questioned if and when it was all going to end. Was Southampton going to be destroyed street by street? It was all so much a matter of chance as well, for across at Northam Road you could still buy high-class confectionery at the Corner Shop, no more than slightly damaged. Mrs Bloomfield's, around the corner, was still offering a hair cut for gentlemen at 6d or one for ladies at 8d. In truth, the German aircraft were not really intent on destroying the Corner Shop. The nameplate on the shop, Northam Road, gives the clue as to their probable target - the Northam yards of Thornycroft & Co. Here repairs were carried out on some 12 million tons gross of merchant shipping in the course of the war. Engineers turned out turbines, boilers, condensers, machinery and electrical equipment for ships, as well as parts for depth charges, torpedoes and mines.

It might be said that the period known as *the phoney war* ended for Southampton in the early hours of June 20th 1940. The first air raid took place, with a total of 10 bombs falling along Regent's Park, South Mill, Millbrook and Westbury Roads. The White House Garage suffered a direct hit on its petrol pumps, causing a huge fire. A damaged water main poured its contents into a bomb crater, closing the main road to Bournemouth. There were no deaths, but six were seriously injured. Those are the cold statistics; the photograph shows some of the reality behind them. Clare House, a confectionery shop belonging to Edith Marshall, has sustained considerable damage, with masses of debris both in the shop window and down the side of the building. Curious passers-by examine the scene with morbid

fascination. If they were at all apprehensive, they were right to be so, for Southampton was to present many scenes far worse than this in the next few months. A serious problem was the number of children back in town. On September 1st and 2nd 1939 many Southampton schoolchildren had been evacuated into North Hampshire and Dorset. Seeming lack of danger had caused a steady drift back. Now another wave of evacuations began.

Events of the 1940s

HOT OFF THE PRESS
At the end of World War II in 1945 the Allies had their first sight of the unspeakable horrors of the Nazi extermination camps they had only heard of until then. In January, 4,000 emaciated prisoners more dead than alive were liberated by the Russians from Auschwitz in Poland, where three million people, most of them Jews, were murdered. The following year 23 prominent Nazis faced justice at Nuremberg; 12 of them were sentenced to death for crimes against humanity.

THE WORLD AT LARGE
The desert area of Alamogordo in New Mexico was the scene of the first atomic bomb detonation on July 16, 1945. With an explosive power equal to more than 15,000 tons of TNT, the flash could be seen 180 miles away. President Truman judged that the bomb could secure victory over Japan with far less loss of US lives than a conventional invasion, and on 6th August the first of the new weapons was dropped on Hiroshima. Around 80,000 people died.

ROYAL WATCH
By the end of World War II, the 19-year-old Princess Elizabeth and her distant cousin Lieutenant Philip Mountbatten RN were already in love. The King and Queen approved of Elizabeth's choice of husband, though they realised that she was rather young and had not mixed with many other young men. The engagement announcement was postponed until the Princess had spent four months on tour in Africa. The couple's wedding on 20th November 1947 was a glittering occasion - the first royal pageantry since before the war.

Above: A forlorn scene meets the eye, offering little more than wreckage along the western side of London Road, looking towards the Civic Centre. The photograph was taken on December 1st 1940 by Ernest Philipps, a nationally known photographer who spent the war years in Southampton and took many such photographs. Saturday, November 23rd 1940, and the following weekend, marked the peak of the Southampton blitz. These three days saw over 1600 high explosive bombs fall, along with around 13,000 incendiaries. Over 200 were killed, and something like 400 were seriously injured. Over 450 properties were completely flattened, and many thousands suffered damage of varying degrees. The nights of November 30th and December 1st were particularly severe, with German bombers arriving in relays. The frontage of Lloyds Bank is visible in the picture, but little remains to suggest that Dibben's ironmongery shop once stood there, or Turner's grocery business. The terrifying new feature of these particular November attacks was the apparently indiscriminate pounding of the historic and commercial centre of the town, linked with attacks on the more usual `military' targets of factories and the docks. Pursuing war by causing maximum civilian terror, a process begun by Hitler in September 1940 with the London blitz, had hit Southampton with a vengeance.

Right: High Street, Above Bar, East Park Terrace - these were some of the casualties of the Southampton blitz of late November and early December 1940. Much of the heart of the town was laid waste. As the photograph shows, there was little left of 83 High Street, premises shared by G J Tilling (sailmakers) and E P Terry, the consul for Costa Rica. The pattern was the same in these heavy raids - flares, followed by incendiary bombs and high explosives. The incendiaries caused fires to rage out of control until the centre of Southampton resembled an inferno. The over-stretched Fire Department simply could not cope as the principal water mains were put out of action by bombs. Despite the assistance of 500 auxiliary firefighters from places as far afield as Ipswich and Peterborough, many detached and semi-detached houses simply had to be left to burn in order that water might be saved for more congested districts. The morning of December 2nd 1940 found Southampton a town without gas, practically without telephone communications, and lacking water or electricity over large areas. Thousands of stunned citizens headed for rescue centres or streamed out of the town looking for safety in the countryside. The worst was over; but no one knew it.

Left: Two children pose rather proudly at the porch, and perhaps for them it was all rather exciting. Nevertheless there is a suspicious looking trench in the garden, much of the fence has gone, and flying debris has done some damage to the porch roof and a window. The date and exact location of this wartime photograph is unknown, but it does illustrate that Hitler's bombs did not recognise social distinctions. They could hit semi-detached houses in pleasant, tree fringed suburbs as well as congested terraced housing near the docks. Perhaps it was a failure to recognise this that explains the presence of the children on the photograph. Even before the outbreak of war, on September 1st and 2nd 1939, many children had been evacuated in school parties to Dorset and North Hampshire. Most of these were from the vulnerable industrialised areas of Southampton. Understandably, parents in the safer suburbs often opted to keep their children with them. To make matters worse, because bombs did not fall on Southampton until June 1940, many of the evacuees returned, their parents having been lulled into a false sense of security. A second wave of evacuations began from June 1940, reaching crisis proportions after the Southampton blitz at the end of November, when adults joined the exodus.

Above: The date and place of this shot is unknown, but what was once fine, suburban property has been devastated. The cross-sectioning of the building on the right has produced a dolls-house effect, with the interior open for inspection. Rather touchingly, a cot and a bed stand side-by-side, the wall they once rested securely against completely gone. Whilst workmen and a warden sift through the rubble, it is possibly some of the former residents who cluster together anxiously on the right. Before the war there was some reluctance among people to accept that bombs might fall on residential areas. The government and local authorities tried to persuade people to prepare. For example Anderson Shelters were made available free to Southampton householders with incomes below £250 per annum. These were dug deep into gardens, leaving a semi-circle of corrugated metal, reinforced by sandbags, above ground. Factories and schools had their own air raid shelters, and public ones were built. Curiously, some of the oldest parts of the town provided the safest refuges, for example the shelters at Bargate and the Medieval Undercroft, the latter being at the corner of Simnel Street and Upper Bugle Street. But some who had witnessed falling debris turning air raid shelters into tombs, preferred to seek safety by trekking into the countryside.

Below: Some astonishing sums of money were raised during the great drives to persuade people to buy such things as War Bonds during the conflict of 1939 to 1945. Southampton's turn to host a Wings for Victory week came between May 22nd and 29th 1943, with a target of £1,100,000 in savings. The indicator at the Civic Centre showed the running total. Posting this figure daily was a ceremonial affair, seen here taking place on May 28th, under the command of Colonel Eric G Brown. The week had been launched by a grand parade and a speech from Air Chief Marshall Sir Philip Joubert. The parade naturally had an RAF flavour, with units of the Fleet Air Arm and Royal Marines participating, amongst others. The RAF on the Target exhibition comprised about 60 pictures of bomb damaged German cities. A Spitfire was on display in the forecourt of the Art Gallery, and the interior could be viewed with the purchase of a savings stamp. Various activities throughout the week, such as concerts and cricket matches, helped to keep the momentum going, and it was announced the following Saturday that the target had been smashed. This achievement is best evaluated by the fact that schoolchildren raised £1 per head - an amazing sum for the 1940s.

> *During World War I, demands on manpower brought women out of their homes*

Right: Women in uniform became a familiar sight during World War II, and these lady drivers have taken time off from their duties to pose for the camera. The girls on the flanks look smart and cheerful, but the figure in the centre provides something of a mystery, for apart from the hat her clothes appear to have a civilian cut about them. The picture was taken in May 1943, and the hooded headlight of the car was necessary as part of blackout regulations. Wars can have positive sides, and both world wars did something to advance the position of women in British society. During World War I, demands on manpower for the front line had brought women out of their homes to work in munitions factories, take on men's jobs and swell the ranks of the nursing profession. By the time of World War II, however, auxiliary units for women had been set up for all branches of the armed services, and women got into military uniform. By repute, the army's Auxiliary Territorial Service (ATS) was the least glamorous, but the Women's Royal Naval Service (WRNS) held great appeal, and this must have been particularly so in Southampton. Whatever the uniform, it enabled women to lead new lives and broaden their horizons.

Where following the right course is the most enjoyable way to success

DEMAND FOR TECHNICAL EDUCATION

St. Mary's Institution to be Used as College

SOUTHAMPTON Education Committee's decision to convert the blitz-damaged St. Mary's Institution into a technical college was the subject of an explanatory statement by Alderman Lewis, chairman of the committee, to the Borough Council.

In recent years, he pointed out, there had been a great development in technical education, and under the new Education Act the Government stressed the need for such education. One of the reasons for the exceptional grants was to produce trained experts, so that Britain could maintain her position in the industrial world.

LOCAL PROGRESS

Development locally had been remarkable. Southampton established a building school in 1945, and its progress had been extraordinary. It had already been changed from a junior to a senior technical school under the 1944 Act.

There were now 1,179 students between the ages of 14 and 27 attending the part-time classes, and 543 between 14 and 57 attending the evening classes. There was likely to be further expansion. It would soon be necessary to transfer from University College to other technical schools the junior trainees sent there. Eastern District School and the Southern District School were both being used for technical studies, and still more accommodation was needed.

"A SENSIBLE THING"

One point of view might be that the Education Committee had acted hastily, but the speaker thought the Council would recognise that they had done a sensible thing. It might be pointed out by some that St. Mary's Institution had been available for a long time. The Housing Committee had thought it could be used for housing people, but found the cost of conversion too great. It was then partially developed for light industries, and two or three were already established there. They would be allowed to remain.

COLLEGE—NOT YET

"There is no chance of getting a new technical college for a long time," said Alderman Lewis. "It will cost probably £200,000, and it may be 10 years before it is built."

Stressing that he could not agree more strongly with everything that had been said about the need for extending technical education, Councillor Burrow objected to the manner in which the matter had been dealt with. He suggested that the Council should have been given at least two weeks to go into the matter.

UNKNOWN QUANTITIES

There were too many unknown quantities about the whole thing. His party was not opposed to technical colleges, and entered only a formal objection to the way the thing had been dealt with.

Councillor W. Lewis protested against the speed with which the matter had been dealt with, describing it as almost a stampede.

It was pointed out by Councillor Mrs. Cutler that the whole thing would have to go back to the Public Assistance Committee, so that no one need be worried about the suggested haste.

Alderman Lewis welcomed the "eleventh hour repentance" of the Ratepayers' Party in not opposing the development of technical education.

The scheme was adopted

Southampton City College plays an important role within the community today. Its history is one of steady growth for around half a century, and over that time the identity of the College has become more clearly defined and its range of courses has become wider so that its students emerge well-equipped to face the challenges of life in the second millennium.

Prior to its change of name on 22nd June 1995, Southampton City College was known as Southampton Technical College. The official opening ceremony of the Technical College took place in 1952, but the origins of the institution can be traced back still further: firstly to a letter written on 16th February 1943 by the Board of Education in Belgrave Square, London, confirming that 'the Board are prepared to recognise . . . a Junior Technical School', and secondly, to the initial intake of students in January 1943. In that month some 50 boys between 13 and 15 years of age enrolled at the new Junior Technical School, located in the Southampton District School at Albert Road and run by Mr Frank Thomas West, former head of the building department of Gloucester Technical College.

The war had brought increased concerns over the country's skills shortage and emphasised the need for more technical education. The School set out to provide a two-year full-time course for boys aged 13 to 15, subsequently adding more part-time and evening courses to its list and taking over the

Above left: *This article, dating from April 1947 shows the intention of the Borough to transform St Mary's Institution into a college.* ***Below:*** *St Mary's Institution during the transformation.* ***Bottom:*** *...and after.*

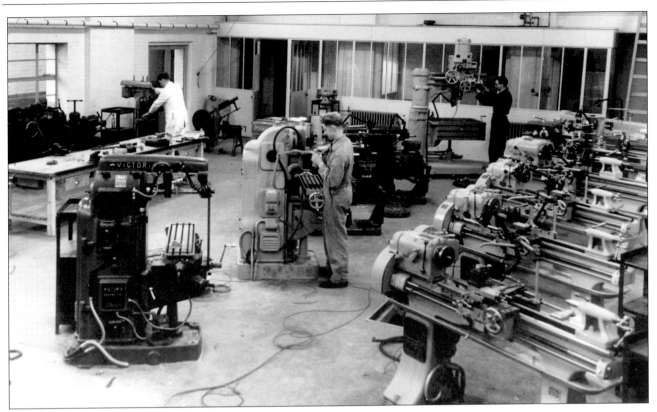

obtained a thorough grounding in 'mathematics, science and drawing office practice, as well as instruction in erection work, metalwork, plumbing, carpentry and joinery. Courses for apprentices are also held throughout the week not only in building but in preliminary engineering, and classes for adult craftsmen are held on Saturday afternoons.' The following year the senior and advanced building courses were revised in accordance with the new syllabuses set by the City & Guilds of London Institute and other examining bodies, and out of the candidates entered for the CGLI examinations by the Technical School, more than half obtained first-class passes. The excellence of the work of the School and its importance to national industry as well as to the students themselves was by now widely recognised.

It was natural that Southampton's new and successful Technical School should feature prominently in the local Education Committee's plans for the future provision of education, and after the war, when the Ministry of Education issued a circular requiring the preparation of development schemes for further education, the Committee was ready with its proposals. It had already identified a potential site for the Technical School - the premises of the former St Mary Street Institution, or Workhouse, situated not far from the School's existing accommodation. This building had sustained considerable damage during the war. However, as it had no permanent occupants and as plans to convert it into flats had been abandoned in favour of tentative plans to turn it over to light industrial use, the Education Committee took advantage of the indecision and proposed that it should be used for educational purposes. While it recognised that the old workhouse, with its small rooms, was not ideal, and that considerable expenditure would be necessary on repairs, improvements to 'artificial light and sanitation' and structural alterations, the Committee nonetheless saw this as the only available means of making 'adequate provision for the growing requirements of further education ' . . . 'pending the erection of a new

running of day-release courses for the building and motor trades from the University College. In 1944 a Pre-Nursing course was established for girls leaving the 'senior elementary schools'; accommodated in temporary war-time buildings in Highfield, this began as a one-year course and developed into a three-year course. The School of Bakery was opened in Swaythling in November 1946, in a former Emergency Feeding Centre; in that year, too, a course in timber technology was established, and moves were made to increase the provision of courses for young women. However, Building seems to have remained an important and very popular area of study for many years.

On 1st April 1945 the Institution officially became a Secondary Technical School, and a feature published in the Daily Echo that month included photographs of Building students at work, and neatly summed up the training provided by the School. During their two years there, boys

Above: The results of cooking courses for girls.
Top: The Machine Shop in December 1950 in the old Chapel.

Technical College'. And so in 1948 the Education Authority took over the old St Mary Workhouse, which, after extensive renovation, became the Technical College.

For the St Mary Street Institution, its new role as the home of the Technical College marked the beginning of a new phase in what had already been a long and eventful existence. The land which the building occupies had a long tradition of care for the sick, the poor and the infirm, having been the site of almshouses since the 17th century. The Institution was built in 1866 to replace an existing workhouse where conditions had been giving rise to concern for some years. Whilst its capacity of 220 inmates had no doubt been perfectly adequate at the time of its construction in 1776, the population of Southampton had increased; and by 1843, with four to a bed, it had already been deemed to be overcrowded. In 1865 it had attracted further criticism from a visiting Poor Law inspector for mixing together in the same room 'all classes, including old, infirm and idiots.' ('Classes' does not refer here to social standing, but to how inmates were classed - the able, the aged, idiots, lunatics, those with skin diseases, those with infectious diseases, married couples, the disorderly, etc.) So a competition was held among local architects, and a Mr T A Skelton's design won. In a style described by the Southampton Times as 'Italian', it conformed with recommendations laid down for the construction of military hospitals. The very detailed description given in the Southampton Times gives the impression of a very spacious edifice, with separate blocks

and individual buildings for specific purposes, but it appears that some of the ratepayers who took up the Council's invitation to visit the new workhouse as it neared completion in November 1868 complained that it was still not large enough. There were also complaints of extravagance in the use of materials such as bath stone and white brick, and indeed the total cost of £30,300 was undeniably in excess of the estimated cost of £19,534. However, much of the overspend was attributed to unforeseen difficulties inherent in the site itself as, when the buildings which had previously occupied the site were pulled down, the ground was apparently 'honeycombed in every direction with old

Above: Construction students at work.
Top: Early cookery classes.

sewers and holes. These had to be filled up with concrete to a depth of 12 or 13 feet before building could commence and a great deal of extra costs were incurred.' One wonders how the previous building had managed to stand up at all.

A number of documents dating back to the early days of the workhouse survived and have been preserved by City College, and these make fascinating reading. They tell us, for instance, about the diet which a Casual Pauper could expect upon admission into the Casual Ward. Adults (aged over 15) who remained in the Ward for one night only received bread (8oz or 6oz for males, 6oz for females) and one pint of either gruel or broth for supper, and the same again for breakfast, children aged between seven and 15 received the same allowance as an adult female, and children aged under seven received 4oz of bread and half a pint of gruel or broth. Those who stayed for more than one night could have either an ounce and a half of cheese or a pint of soup with their bread (again, with smaller quantities for the under-sevens). A one-night stay appears to have entailed three hours' work, while a full day's work consisted of nine hours - males could spend their nine hours breaking stones, while work for females could take the form of washing, scrubbing and cleaning. The punishment for offences such as absconding or refusing to work is also described, and a very important factor here was whether the offender was classed as 'a rogue and vagabond' or simply as

an idle and disorderly person - if the first, he or she was liable to be sentenced to three months' imprisonment with hard labour, while the second category escaped with only one month's imprisonment with hard labour.

The workhouse system was superseded by National Assistance on 31st March 1930, by which time a number of extensions had been added to the main building since the time of its construction. National Assistance looked after the needs of the poor between 1930 and 1946, and the old workhouse appeared in the 1946 street directory as 'County Borough of Southampton Public Assistance Committee Relief Offices'. During the war the building, no doubt because of its size, had been pressed into service in a variety of ways, including being used as an emergency food centre and for housing homeless families. Five of its blocks survived the wartime bombing, and it was subsequently agreed that the building should be handed over to the Education Authority. On 31st October 1949, with reconstruction still in progress, the Technical College held its first classes in the former St Mary's Workhouse, and a new era began.

Preliminary estimates put the cost of clearing away debris, making the building safe and carrying out minimal redeco-

Above: *The notification of some of the College's courses in 1953.*
Below: *The staff in the 1950s.*

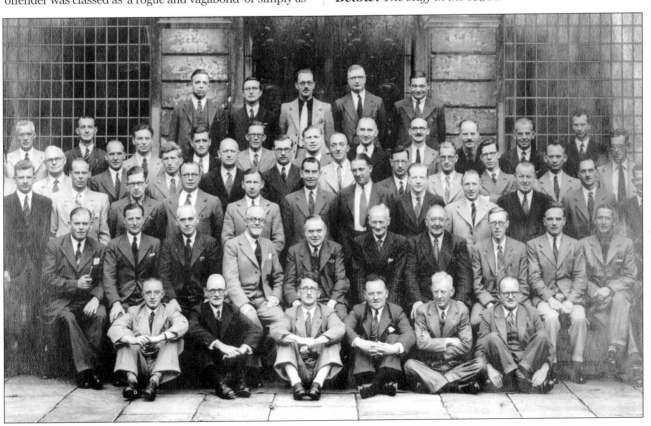

ration and internal structural alterations would be £22,003, although it was hoped to claim some £15,000 back from the War Damage Commission. This inevitably meant financial constraints, but the College had already developed considerable expertise in finding ingenious and money-saving ways around such limitations. By the beginning of 1949, the Albert Road premises' 18 class-rooms and science laboratories, together with such other accommodation as the College had been able to acquire, were housing around 3,000 students aged between 15 and 50-plus, attending full-time, part-time and evening classes - a significant increase in numbers from the 50 students the Junior Technical School had enrolled in the same premises six years previously! An enthusi-astic spirit of invention reigned in the workshops, with students persuading local people to give them second-hand tools and equipment, and finding imaginative ways to transform scrap material into functional apparatus: the landing gear of an old Spitfires became a hydraulic crane model, more Spitfire components combined with oxygen bottles became a complete modern water softening plant and a prefab heating plant. The students also made an item which they described as a 'roof truss stress gauge' from scrap rescued from a Corporation dump, and this aroused the interest of building and technical experts all over the country, who requested details of the design. It is not surprising that such an active and dynamic student community should obtain excellent results, and indeed Southampton Technical College achieved some remarkable examination successes. For instance, four special prizes were offered by the Lead Manufacturers' Association and

Copper Development Association for the two national plumbing examinations which were sat by candidates from every technical college in Great Britain in 1949, and three of these four prizes went to students of Southampton Technical College. This brought the College much well-deserved praise from the Education Committee, and already it was generally recognised that the institution, relatively new though it was - by 1949 its very first cohort of students had barely finished their apprenticeships - had an important part to play in the future of Southampton.

By the time St Mary's Workhouse was acquired for the College's use, the need for additional premises had become acute. The former Southern District School in Latimer

Above: The standard of education was always high.
Below: ...and at the forefront of modern technology.

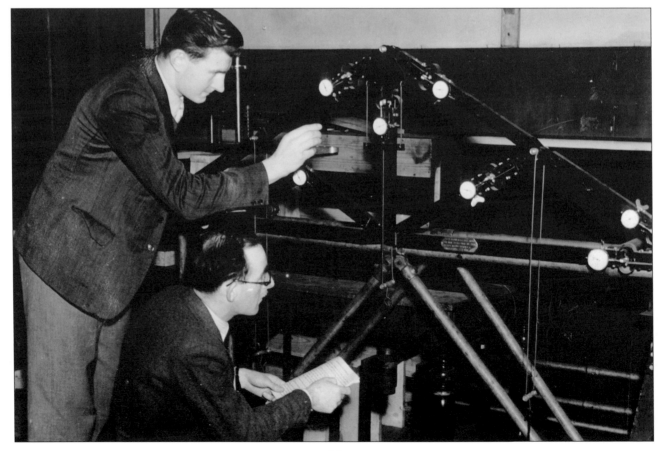

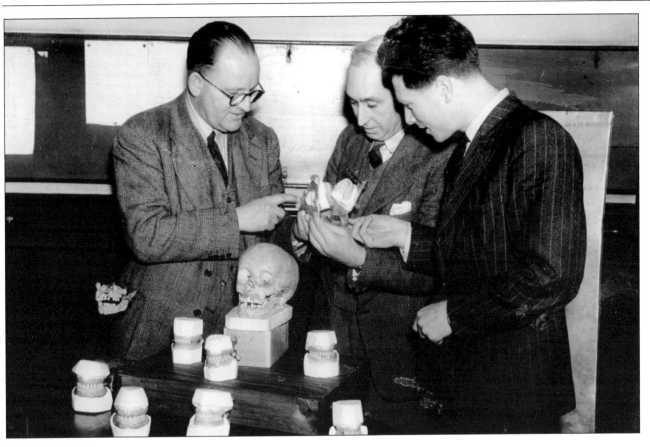

Street was being used in addition to the Albert Street buildings, but as the College's course provision increased, much more space was needed. Building courses and junior engineering classes up to the level of the Ordinary National Certificate had been transferred to the Technical College from University College (now Southampton University), and the Building courses in particular had expanded greatly within a very short time; additionally, entirely new courses such as Electrical Installation and Yacht and Boat Building had been established, while September 1951 saw the transfer of all commercial teaching from University College to the Technical College. The Official Opening of the St Mary Street Premises took place on 27th June 1952, and the ceremony was performed by Mr F Bray CB, Under Secretary to the Ministry of Education. Although the scheme was at this time only half completed, a tremendous amount of work had been carried out: the front block of buildings, which had been damaged in the war, had been removed, together with the storehouses and the stone-breaking cells behind it, the doctor's house had been restored and turned into the Caretaker's house, and teaching accommodation included an engineering machine shop, workshops, laboratories and drawing offices; practical rooms and a model

'house' for Domestic Science teaching; classrooms, lecture rooms, common rooms, a library, an assembly hall and administration offices.

Over the years which followed further building work was carried out at St Mary Street, and the range of courses available at the Technical College continued to expand. Courses on offer for session 1953-54 covered everything from Baking and Confectionery to Dental Technicians' Work, and from Elements of English Law to Municipal and Sanitary Engineering. By 1960 part-time student numbers had reached 8,000, and in addition there were more than a thousand full-time students; by 1964 there were 11,000 students. In 1960 work had begun on a new College of Technology, with the intention of relieving some of the

Above: *In 1998 the Princess Royal visited the College to open its new £2.7 million resource building.*
Top: *Students' work under scrutiny.*
Left: *A modern-day carpenter at work.*

pressure on the existing College, but this was not completed for almost a decade. So the Technical College made use of any available buildings, such as nearby Chantry Hall and Central Hall, and continued to meet the city's needs almost single-handedly until complementary provision could be made. The man who was responsible for building up the College in its first two decades, principal F T West, was honoured by the award of an MBE in 1954, in recognition of his services to technical education. Mr West retired in 1964 - and all readers who have close connections with the College will no doubt remember that he celebrated his 100th birthday with a slap-up meal in the College's restaurant at the end of April 1999!

The College's next major organisational change came about on 1st April 1969. Prior to that it had been administered as part of the Southampton College of Technology; it now became a separate entity, and as such it adopted the name of The Southampton Technical College. Under its new name it continued to grow; 1973 saw the opening of a new Food Trades Block, and gradually the wide range of courses and the excellent facilities which we associate with this institution today began to take shape. Nineteen seventy-nine was a year for special celebration; not only did the College reach its 30th year at its current site, but its main building, the former workhouse, reached the age of 100.

On 22nd June 1995 the College changed its name to Southampton City College, a designation which better reflects the forward-thinking range of courses currently on offer to people in and

Above: The Reception of the College Library. Right: Modernday computer-aided design classes.

around the city. Its part-time courses take place at 15 centres in Southampton, and are run at weekends as well as in the evening and during the day, so that students can arrange their study hours round their other commitments. Facilities are continually being extended and improved; at the time of writing City College is looking forward to the completion of its new state-of-the-art Hair and Beauty Suite, and it has recently invested in a Community Theatre and a Nursery - named Sunrise - while its multi-million pound, multi-media resources centre, opened by HRH Princess Anne in May 1998, is one of the best in the South of England. Another of the College's distinctions is its Engineering Centre of Excellence status; Tony Roche, Vice President of the Institution of Mechanical Engineers, visited City College on 30th April 1999 to open one of the most-up-to-date engineering facilities in the region, representing an investment of nearly half a million pounds by the College and equipped with the latest technology including CAD/CAM facilities. City College operates in partnership with seven other institutions in

Hampshire, with each centre focusing on a different area of engineering, so that small to medium-sized businesses in the county can train staff and fill the skills gap created as technology advances.

Students of Southampton City College have a long tradition of outstanding success, from the proud plumbers who scooped three out of four national prizes in 1949 to the three trainee chefs who won the prestigious Nestle Toque d'Or contest in 1999, while another former student whose activities have brought him international fame - and who would no doubt approve wholeheartedly of the activities of the new Community Theatre - is that master of controversy and film director extraordinaire, Ken Russell. But there are many

thousands of contented former students whose studies have brought simply the quiet satisfaction of having learned a new skill, developed an existing talent, improved their career prospects, added a new dimension to their life or achieved a lifelong personal ambition. City College's Community Team is working hard to spread the message that learning is for everyone. There are car maintenance classes for women, free basic skills courses for those whose reading, writing and arithmetic could be improved, and a range of IT classes covering everything from a gentle introduction to using a computer to surfing the Internet. In fact, whatever you want to do, Southampton City College is the place where you can learn to do it (within reason, of course!).

Southampton City College's most famous son once said that 'success in art is 90 per cent drudgery'. Far be it from us to disagree with Ken Russell, but 'drudgery' is hardly an accurate description of work at City College. With modern facilities, a refurbished Student Guidance Centre, and a range of courses designed to meet the needs and wishes of the community, Southampton City College's aim is to help all its students to both enjoy their studies and to succeed, in a supportive and caring environment. It is an aim in which the College has achieved admirable success for more than half a century, and one which it will continue to fulfil well into the future.

Left: *Hairdressing in the College's salons.*
Below: *The College today.*

On the move

Events of the 1940s

INVENTION AND TECHNOLOGY

Inspired by quick-drying printers' ink, in 1945 Hungarian journalist Laszlo Biro developed a ballpoint pen which released viscous ink from its own reservoir as the writer moved the pen across the page. An American inventor was working on a similar idea at the same time, but it was Biro's name that stuck. A few years later Baron Bich developed a low cost version of the pen, and the 'Bic' ballpoint went on sale in France in 1953.

SCIENCE AND DISCOVERY

In 1943 Ukrainian-born biochemist Selman Abraham Waksman made a significant discovery. While studying organisms found in soil he discovered an antibiotic (a name Waksman himself coined) which was later found to be the very first effective treatment for tuberculosis. A major killer for thousands of years, even the writings of the ancient Egyptians contain stories of people suffering from tuberculosis. Waksman's development of strepto-mycin brought him the 1952 Nobel Prize for Medicine.

A tricky operation for the crane operator, but there seem to be plenty of people on hand to give advice. At first sight it is unclear as to whether this locomotive is being winched into or out of the hold. However, as the picture was taken in August 1947, probably it was heading for the USA, for although the locomotive was of the Empire Baltic (War Department) Class, it had *US Army* painted on the side. Before the war, shunting within the docks was done by a number of small tank engines specially designed to cope with the sharp curves leading on to the quays. As the port became heavily involved in the preparations for the invasion of Europe, these engines were overwhelmed by the enormous increase in docks traffic. Therefore, as early as 1942, larger locomotives began to arrive, imported by United States Army Transport. There were 14 in all, and they proved themselves to be so useful in the docks that they were purchased and retained by the Southern Railway after the war.

From the falling of the first German bombs on Southampton, in June 1940, to the time of the final attack, in July 1944, the South Western Hotel led a charmed life. In spite of its huge bulk, making it seemingly an easy target for enemy aircraft, somewhat like St Paul's in London the hotel emerged almost unscathed whilst havoc was being wreaked all around it. This is all the more surprising when one considers that the hotel was situated close to the docks, the Southampton Terminus station and the railway shunting yard. Even at the peak of the local blitz, the final two weekends of November 1940 when 250 were killed and 400 seriously injured, the South Western got through. How close a thing it was, however, is illustrated by the picture, taken on the first of those two terrible Saturdays, November 23rd 1940. Clear evidence of bomb damage lies all around, from the roof of a station building to the debris being transferred from the road to the back of a wagon. For much of the war the hotel housed the local headquarters staff of the Admiralty and Army Movement Control, and was used in the naval preparations for D-Day. Somebody in high places must have known something!

the Royal Pier. Perhaps, after all, the photograph should be regarded as a cheering one. By April the worst was over, and this train was carrying much needed goods to the rest of Britain.

Top: The massive shape of the South Western Hotel shares the background with dock cranes, whilst in the foreground an engine gently simmers in Southampton Terminus Station. All three elements in this photograph of around 1960 were

Above: Do you view this as a memento to the glorious age of steam, or do you see it as a bleak scene, with a dirty steam engine pouring out smoke and soot? There may be a bit of truth in both viewpoints. The engine provides an arresting picture of power and strength as it hauls its train of freight wagons out of Southampton docks in April 1947. On the other hand the scenario might be regarded as bleak because 1947 saw Britain in the grip of post-war austerity. The end of World War II in 1945 did not miraculously end shortages. All manner of goods were still scarce. Rationing continued for food as late as 1954 in these drab post-war years. To make matters worse, just about the worst winter in living memory hit Britain in early 1947, and for over two months the country froze up. As inland transport broke down, the electricity generating stations were starved of coal, leading to power cuts. Southampton experienced nine inches of snow in seven days in January. On February 28th a one inch thick ice floe was seen near

intimately bound up with each other. The hotel was built alongside the station in 1872, beginning its life as the Imperial Hotel, and being renamed the South Western Hotel in the 1880s. Its function was to serve Southampton's growing business in rail and ship passenger services. The station had been opened in 1840, and for some time it was Southampton's only station, providing a terminus for London trains, although boat trains ran directly into the docks from their own special junction. The station's name evolved from simply being Southampton in 1840 to Southampton Docks in 1858. It finally adopted the title Terminus in 1923. The station dealt in a large fish traffic, and as late as 1965 it handled an average of 85 passenger trains per day. However, passengers per train were very few and the station was closed in 1966. The old grandeur of the South Western Hotel went in much the same way. Its change to South Western House saw it become an accommodation block for offices and studios.

Two well-known names in their own right make an appearance in this 1950s photograph. *Buy Your Oil the Safe Way* is the invitation on the side of the Andrews vehicle, which has all the appearance of being one of the company's mobile refuellers. The Andrews business set up at Southampton Docks in 1920 and is still going strong today as Andrews (Shipside) Services. As well as providing dockside fuel for motorists, Andrews is well-known for providing storage facilities for passengers who wish to leave their cars at the Port. The other well-known name is that of Arundel Castle, one of the foremost liners of the Union Castle Line. The company ran the Royal Mail service to South and East Africa, for which Arundel Castle began her service in 1921. She began as a four-funnel

steamer, but after a 1937 refit in Belfast she emerged as the handsome, two-funnel ship of the photograph. Not long afterwards Arundel Castle found herself carrying troops, and in this respect she had a long war, carrying over 200,000 men, and not returning to Union Castle until 1950. In 1958, after long service in carrying mail, cargo and passengers, this ever popular ship finally left Southampton, bound for a scrapyard in Hong Kong.

Events of the 1950s

WHAT'S ON?
Television hit Britain in a big way during the 1950s. Older readers will surely remember 'Double Your Money, Dixon of Dock Green and 'Dragnet' (whose characters' names were changed 'to protect the innocent'). Commercial television was introduced on 22nd September 1955, and Gibbs SR toothpaste were drawn out of the hat to become the first advert to be shown. Many believed adverts to be vulgar, however, and audiences were far less than had been hoped for.

GETTING AROUND
The year 1959 saw the development of the world's first practical air-cushion vehicle - better known to us as the hovercraft. The earliest model was only able to travel at slow speeds over very calm water and was unable to carry more than three passengers. The faster and smoother alternative to the sea ferry quickly caught on, and by the 1970s a 170-ton car-carrying hovercraft service had been introduced across the English Channel.

SPORTING CHANCE
The four-minute mile had remained the record since 1945, and had become regarded as virtually unbreakable. On 6th May 1954, however, Oxford University student Roger Bannister literally ran away with the record, accomplishing the seemingly impossible in three minutes 59.4 seconds. Bannister collapsed at the end of his last amazing lap, even temporarily losing his vision. By the end of the day, however, he had recovered sufficiently to celebrate his achievement in a London night club!

Above: Ocean Terminal was opened in 1950, and judging by the appearance of the vehicles on view this picture dates from the early years of the following decade. Sightseeing is the order of the day, both from the open-top bus and the visitors' balcony of Ocean Terminal building. Queen Mary is obviously the great attraction. She had the kind of reputation that meant if you could not afford the glamorous experience of sailing on her, at least a bit of the magic rubbed off if you saw her, and you could tell people you had seen her. There would be plenty of statistics to absorb, along with those little human interest angles so beloved of tour guides. Queen Mary, launched in 1934 with a gross tonnage of 81,000; 10 million rivets used in her construction; the cost for a Southampton to New York return ticket in the 1930s - Cabin Class £102, Tourist £52 10s, Third Class £33 10s. Presumably Cunard White Star had Cabin Class passengers in mind when it decided to install a dog promenade deck and a lamp post in the kennels! In spite of all the luxury, the Atlantic could still have the last say. In its early days the ship tended to roll badly in heavy seas, reducing furniture to matchwood.

Above right: The dash for the sun is on as passengers queue to board a British United Airways holiday flight at Southampton Airport. Judging by their warm outer clothing it is not summer, and so this might represent a welcome winter break. British United Airways might have disappeared, but the social revolution caused by the rise of air travel continues. In one sense there is no holiday season now, just peaks, for planes are as likely to be as full at Christmas as in midsummer. What a far cry from the days when holidays were linked solely to fairs and religious festivals, and were as regular as the rhythm of the agricultural seasons. Southampton's oldest fair in this respect was Trinity Fair, a five day event dating back to at least the 15th century. The railway age brought day-tripping or longer stays within the reach of ordinary people, and so places such as Bournemouth, Brighton and Weymouth grew into holiday resorts. Sotonians could also enjoy the steam packets going to the Isle of Wight or France, and the first steamer service to Le Havre opened up in 1823. And so to charter flights and long-hauls, a weekend in Rome or a month in Australia - a world away from shinning up the greasy pole at Trinity Fair!

Below: Between 1938 and 1950, with a break for the war, Imperial Airways sent a fleet of flying boats around the world in the service of its Empire Air Mail Scheme. The photograph shows one of the `C' class flying boats `Circe,' at berth 108, with a warship in the background. World War I had seen great strides made in the development of aircraft, and further improvements were stimulated by international competition for the Schneider Trophy. This was the Blue Ribbon of the Air, and in the 1920s Britain won the trophy four times with seaplanes designed by R J Mitchell and built at the Supermarine Works, Southampton. Increasing speeds were reached, and in 1929 Mitchell's S6 set up a new world speed record of 357.7 mph. The Vickers-Supermarine S6B had pushed this speed up to 407.5 mph by 1931. To most people the Schneider Trophy was simply a matter of international prestige, but Mitchell realised that air power was the key to supreme military power. From this belief was born

Mitchell's masterpiece, the `Spitfire,' the saviour of the country during the Battle of Britain. Built by Vickers-Supermarine at Southampton, the fuselage of the prototype, test-piloted in 1936, carried the unmistakable lines of those all-conquering British seaplanes.

Bottom: Improvements in design and speed helped to foster a commercial role for flying boats. The first regular services, to Guernsey in the Channel Islands, were begun in 1923. Part of this operation involved Supermarine Aviation, who built seaplanes at their factories at Hythe and Woolston. Imperial Airways (which became part of BOAC in 1940) took over the Guernsey venture in 1924, although this pioneer service only lasted until 1929. What really ushered in the golden age of the flying boat in commercial terms was the Empire Air Mail Scheme from 1934, based at Southampton. Imperial Airways ordered 28 C class monoplanes, and the maiden departure of the

service was in June 1937. Passengers and mail departed from Southampton for Durban, South Africa. Berth 108 was soon settled on, and passengers were ferried out by motor launch. The picture shows both passengers and mail in the loading operation on to Centaurus. To travel in this way must have offered a unique thrill, and the destinations were not lacking in ambition - Cairo, Singapore, Sydney. BOAC resumed operations after the war, even opening a new terminal in 1948 at berth 50. Competition from improved long-range land planes, however, caused BOAC to abandon seaplanes in 1950, although Aquila Airways operated from berth 50 until 1958.

Events of the 1950s

HOT OFF THE PRESS
The 1950s seemed to be the heyday of spies, and in 1951 the activities of Guy Burgess and Donald Maclean caused a sensation in the country. Both had occupied prominent positions in the Foreign Office, while Burgess had also been a member of MI-6. Recruited by the Russians while at Cambridge University in the 1930s, the traitors provided the Soviets with a huge amount of valuable information. They disappeared in 1951, surfacing in Moscow five years later.

THE WORLD AT LARGE
Plans to develop the economies of member states into one common market came to fruition on 1st January 1958, when the EEC came into operation. The original members were France, Belgium, Luxembourg, The Netherlands, Italy, and West Germany. The Community became highly successful, achieving increased trade and prosperity across Western Europe while at the same time alleviating fear of war which lingered on after the end of World War II. Britain became a member in 1973.

SCIENCE AND DISCOVERY
DNA (deoxyribonucleic acid) was first defined as long ago as 1953, and the effects have been far-reaching. The key discovery was developed over the following years and today DNA fingerprinting has become an accepted part of life. Genetic diseases such as hemophilia and cystic fibrosis have been identified. Criminals are continually detected and brought to justice. Biological drugs have been developed. More controversially, drought and disease-resistant plants have been engineered - and Dolly the sheep has been produced.

What a delight to the eyes of connoisseurs of transport as two great representatives of rail and sea are caught on the same photograph. Pacific No 34088, 213 Squadron, rests at Ocean Terminal whilst the stately shape of Cunard liner, Queen Elizabeth, dominates the background. For many people the romance of travel would find its ultimate expression here - to be conveyed on a steam-hauled boat train in order to disembark on a luxury liner. The date of the photo-

graph is, however, May 1964 and the end of an era was in sight. Four years later was to mark the end of both the steam age on British Rail and Queen Elizabeth's life as a liner. Ocean Terminal had been opened in 1950 as a state-of-the-art complex worthy of Britain's premier passenger port. It had mechanical conveyors for both passengers and baggage, along with a host of facilities.

Who could have forecast then how soon the rise of air travel would hit the passenger liner business? However, this is what happened, and in 1968 Queen Elizabeth was sold as a tourist attraction to a group of American businessmen. Boat trains declined too, but which Sotonian who ever saw them will forget those aristocrats of steam pulling their Pullman cars into Eastern Docks?

Bird's eye view

> *The Mayflower Plaza has a tradition of theatre going back to 1803*

An immediate impression is created by this aerial view of how much pleasant greenery exists in the heart of Southampton. The Central Parks were established between 1844 and 1866 on the ancient fields known as Lammas Lands. Watts Park is closest to the Civic Centre, which is quite appropriate, for every four hours the clock tower chimes out the hymn, Oh God our help in ages past. These words were written by Isaac Watts, a prominent local Nonconformist minister. Moving from the Civic Centre towards the bottom right-hand corner, one would today enter the Marlands Shopping Centre. The photograph predates its building, and it is interesting to note that the Rose Garden is shown, just below Civic Centre Road. This has now gone, and its fountain can be found in front of the entrance to the Central Library. Towards the bottom left, the railway line is visible before it disappears into the tunnel under the city centre, and a hint of the steam age can be seen. At the very left of the picture, just above the railway, is the site which is now called the Mayflower Plaza. It has a tradition of theatre running back from the Mayflower itself, through the old Empire Theatre to the Theatre Royal, built in 1803.

When Southampton Docks came into existence in 1838
their creators could not have foreseen the shape of
things to come. The amount of land reclaimed from the
River Test is well illustrated in the bottom half of the
shot by the arches of the Arcades, against which the Test
used to lap. St Michael's Church spire stands tall just to
the rear of the Arcades. Moving up the waterfront to the

right of the shot, the large open space before reaching
the Royal Pier is now Mayflower Park, home of the
International Boat Show. The pavilion and a good
portion of Royal Pier were later destroyed by fire but
these features are still present here. Next comes the
Town Quay, with the dome of the Harbour Board
Offices at the landward end. Above that, the

well-known shipbuilding name of Harland & Wolff is visible on the roof of the workshops at No 6 (Trafalgar) Drydock. Beyond Ocean Dock, the buildings of Ocean Terminal protrude seawards. These were created in 1950 and would have been the height of modernity in a view which is probably dated shortly after this. The site of the present day Ocean Village, towards the upper left, was the old Inner and Outer Docks at this date.

Events of the 1950s

MELODY MAKERS
Few teenage girls could resist the blatant sex-appeal of 'Elvis the Pelvis', though their parents were scandalised at the moody Presley's provocatively gyrating hips. The singer took America and Britain by storm with such hits as 'Jailhouse Rock', 'All Shook Up' and 'Blue Suede Shoes'. The rhythms of Bill Haley and his Comets, Buddy Holly, Chuck Berry, and Roy Orbison (who had a phenomenal three-octave voice) turned the 1950s into the Rock 'n' Roll years.

INVENTION AND TECHNOLOGY
Until the late 1950s you did not carry radios around with you. Radios were listened to at home, plugged into a mains socket in every average sitting room. Japan was in the forefront of electronic developments even then, and in 1957 the Japanese company Sony introduced the world's very first all-transistor radio - an item of new technology that was small enough to fit into your pocket. The major consumer product caught on fast - particularly with teenage listeners.

ROYAL WATCH
King George VI's health had been causing problems since 1948, when he developed thrombosis. In 1951 the King - always a heavy smoker - became ill again, and was eventually found to be suffering from lung cancer. His left lung was removed in September of 1951. In January 1952 he waved Princess Elizabeth and Prince Philip off on their tour of Africa; they were never to see him again. The King died on 5th February 1952.

> *The buildings flanking Above Bar were destroyed during the second world war*

Two of the best landmarks in the central part of Southampton seem to stand counterpoised on this aerial shot of 1961. One is the clock tower of the Civic Centre in the top left-hand corner, whilst the other is Bargate in the bottom right-hand corner. The Civic Centre, which was opened in 1938, is shown to good advantage, with the Magistrates Court appearing just in front of the tower. The Library and Art Gallery run along the top side of the complex, facing the greenery of the Central Parks. The long stretch of Portland Terrace runs down the left of the photograph, and the old bus station can be picked out to the right of the top section. Towards the bottom of Portland Terrace, it is an easy matter to trace Bargate Street along to the right, emerging at the famous Bargate itself. This sturdy monument is a reminder that medieval Southampton existed below this point, down to the water's edge, and that Bargate was the northern gateway to the old walled town. The contrast between Bargate's architecture and that of its neighbours became even more stark when most of the traditional buildings flanking Above Bar were destroyed during World War II, enforcing a rebuilding programme.

The words Southampton and docks seem to go hand-in-hand, and in this view of 1924 one's attention is inevitably drawn to the wonderful floating dock in the foreground. The creation of this marvel was another step in the great expansion of the docks after World War I. In the eighteenth century, Southampton's reputation was based on its attractions as a pleasant spa town. The growth of the rail network and the expansion of trade with the Far East opened up great possibilities for Southampton provided that docking facilities were good enough. These were created out of 216 acres of mudland. The official opening, and the beginning of

Southampton as the Gateway to the World, took place on October 12th 1838. Almost 100 years later, expansion had been so great that there was an urgent need for extra drydock facilities to accommodate the various large liners based at Southampton. The huge floating drydock, capable of lifting vessels up to 60,000 tons, was constructed on the Tyne and towed to Southampton. The new dock was 960 feet long and 134 feet wide, and it was operational until 1934. After this, its career took in spells at Portsmouth and Rotterdam (until 1983) before it was wrecked off the Spanish coast whilst under tow.

A sight to stir the soul of all lovers of ships, the magnificent Cunard liner, Mauretania, berthed at Southampton. The photograph dates from the early 1930s, when she had begun her days as a cruise liner. Mauretania was built in 1906 on Tyneside by Swan, Hunter and Wigham Richardson. Her maiden voyage was from Liverpool to New York in 1907, and Liverpool remained her base until replaced by

Southampton in 1920. She broke the record for an Atlantic crossing in 1909, achieving the voyage in 4 days, 17 hours and 20 minutes, a record which she held for 20 years. The first world war brought about a change of role, and Mauretania was refitted as a troopship, mainly for Atlantic trips. There was always fierce competition for passengers on the Atlantic run in peacetime days, and Mauretania was given a degree

Down at the docks

Events of the 1960s

WHAT'S ON?
Television comedy came into its own in the 1960s, and many of the shows that were favourites then went on to become classics. 'On the Buses', 'Steptoe and Son', 'Till Death Us Do Part' and 'The Army Game' kept audiences laughing, while the incredible talents of Morecambe and Wise, the wit of Des O'Connor - often the butt of the duo's jokes - and the antics of Benny Hill established them for ever in the nation's affections.

GETTING AROUND
The 2nd March 1969 was a landmark in the history of aviation. The Anglo-French supersonic airliner Concorde took off for the first time from Toulouse in France. Concorde, which can cruise at almost twice the speed of sound, was designed to fly from London to New York in an incredible three hours twenty minutes. The event took place just weeks after the Boeing 747, which can carry 500 passengers to Concorde's modest 100, made its first flight.

SPORTING CHANCE
Wembley Stadium saw scenes of jubilation when on 30th July 1966 England beat West Germany 4-2 in the World Cup. The match, played in a mixture of sunshine and showers, had been a nailbiting experience for players and spectators alike from the very beginning when Germany scored only thirteen minutes into the game. It was Geoff Hurst's two dramatic goals scored in extra time that secured the victory and lifted the cup for England - at last.

of luxury and comfort which would enable Cunard to compete with rival British companies, such as White Star, and with foreign lines. Her first-class quarters can only be described as sumptuous, with inlaid mahogany panelling and marble fireplaces in the lounge, accompanied by French tapestries. Between 1930 and 1935 Mauretania served as a cruise liner, and there was much sadness when The Grand Old Lady departed for Rosyth to be scrapped in 1935.

Above: The simple pleasures of yesteryear find some expression in this photograph of the Royal Pier, taken around 1908. A pleasant stroll to take the fresh air on the Pier cost only tuppence, although the temptations of the penny slot machines, just beyond the gatehouse, might have taken some resisting. A straight walk up the Pier brought one to the Pavilion, at the far end, the home of dances, concerts and exhibitions. There were plenty of interesting ships to view as well, including paddle steamers such as the one to the left. The Royal Victoria Pier had been opened in 1833 by Princess Victoria. The Southampton Harbour Commissioners had footed the bill of £13,000, the aim being to accommodate steam packets bound for the Isle of Wight and Europe. The simple early structure was enlarged in the early 1890s on a design created by Edward Cooper Poole, winner of the design competition. The gatehouse with its clock tower formed part of the enlargement, as did the Pavilion. The latter became a focal point for entertainment, and was extended in 1922. The Royal Pier was popular enough to warrant its use as a place for advertisements, and they line the railway track which brought passengers right down to the ships.

Above right: Although viewed from a different angle, clearly much has changed on the Royal Pier by the time of the 1930s, the probable era of this photograph. Between 1929 and 1930 the old gatehouse was replaced by a new one. This can clearly be seen on the right, and the only features preserved from the old gatehouse were the heraldic lions. The design belonged very much to its age, but was regarded as vulgar by those who described it as `wedding cake' architecture. Nevertheless it served to publicise the attractions of the Royal Pier well enough. Dancing and concerts were ever popular entertainments in the 1930s, not to mention the archetypal pier entertainment, the Pierrot show. The bracing sea air and a view of fine ships had as much appeal at this time as it had in the Edwardian age, and indeed still has today for Sotonians. The Royal Pier continued to develop after the second world war, with a ballroom installed in the Pier Pavilion in 1963. However, by 1979 the Royal Pier had closed down as an entertainments concern, although the Gatehouse continued in operation for some years to come. Disastrous fires destroyed the Pavilion and much of the far end of the Pier in 1987 and 1992.

The repair men are busy at work in this dramatic shot of the vessel `Hartlepool,' in dry dock at Southampton on October 21st 1940. Enemy action was responsible for some of the damage, although it may be that the repair gang needed to cut sheer through the end of the ship in order to make a clean job. If the docks at Southampton were busy enough before World War II, once the conflict had begun activity reached fever pitch. In 1942, for example, at any one time hundreds of vessels could be found there - cruisers, destroyers, armed merchant ships, minesweepers, landing craft and many other categories. Harland and Wolff were deeply involved in repairs, as well as equipping the first experimental vessel for combating magnetically detonated sea-mines. The Northam yards of John I Thornycroft made repairs to around twelve million tons of merchant shipping during the course of the war, and at Woolston the firm managed to build 17 destroyers, plus many other ships. All this was achieved despite some fierce German air attacks, particularly during 1940 and 1941. Imagination and ingenuity were applied to the task of converting ships for different roles, eg the conversion of merchant ships into troop carriers or hospital ships.

Bottom: The docks as a hive of industry is well illustrated in this 1955 scene. Rails criss-cross the foreground, steam hisses from engines at work and the cranes are busy. Amongst the clusters of sheds, buildings and offices the famous shipbuilding name of Harland and Wolff can be seen on the far right. Almost in the middle of the photograph, berthed at Ocean Dock, is the stately shape of Queen Mary. Ocean Dock had been the renowned terminus of the Cunard and White Star Lines during the golden days of the passenger liners between the war. Of all the illustrious names, those of Queen Mary, along with her sister ship Queen Elizabeth, have the strongest holds on people's imagination. As if the reality of such ships was not epic enough, legends grew about them also. When Cunarder No 534 was built at John Brown & Co at Clydebank, and christened Queen Mary on her launching in 1934, a persistent rumour spread that Cunard had intended to name the ship Victoria, and that the name it received was due to a misunderstanding on the part of King George V. The great ship took up its berth at Southampton and made its maiden voyage on May 27th 1936, sailing to New York.

Right: The death in 1999 of Sir Christopher Cockerell reminded many of the hopes that were once attached to his invention, and perhaps the unfulfilled ambitions. The hovercraft, as featured here in this British Hovercraft Corporation publicity photograph, was Sir Christopher's brainchild. The story of his first experiment bears all the hallmarks of scientific ingenuity applied to simple objects. He blew air from a vacuum cleaner into inverted coffee tins suspended over kitchen scales. From those humble beginnings the hovercraft was developed and the prototype crossed the Channel in two hours and three minutes in 1959. Production forged ahead and optimism was high in the 1960s, although more caution was expressed in the 1970s when unforeseen problems began to arise - corrosion to the gas turbine engines, perishing of the rubber skirting. Nevertheless hovercraft began to compete for a slice of the lucrative cross-Channel ferry traffic, and a Southampton to Cowes Service ran until 1980. Also the Southampton region has been to the fore in the manufacture of hovercraft. In 1994 the 40th anniversary of the hovercraft's invention was celebrated by a parade of 12 hovercraft from the inventor's home at Hythe to HMS Daedalus at Lee-on-Solent. Hovercraft had achieved much, but not as much as he had wanted.

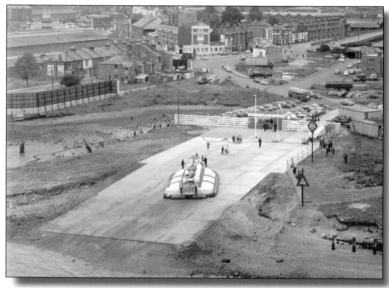

point they provided work for around 12,000 people, with another 35,000 jobs being port-related. Probably, however, the scenes of the most feverish activity at the docks were witnessed when the port became the largest military and naval base of all time, in preparation for Overlord in 1944 - the invasion of occupied Europe. Amongst the massive undertakings were those of building the artificial Mulberry Harbour and creating PLUTO (Pipe Line Under The Ocean).

Top: The sheer scale of the type of work under-taken at the docks is impressively demonstrated by this photograph of a caisson at No 5 Dry Dock. A caisson is the floating part of a dock which acts as a gate. This example may have been under construction or under repair. The scene was captured in former times, but then as now large-scale vision was required for many aspects of dock work. The men seem minute in comparison with the materials they are handling. In such circumstances, precise control and judgement were required from those in charge to avoid disaster. The featured dry dock was opened in 1895 by the Prince of Wales (later to become King Edward VII) and was named after him. No 5 Dry Dock was at the time the largest one in the world. It formed part of an almost continuous process of expansion which had taken place since the opening of Southampton Docks in 1838. Between 1846 and 1879 four graving or dry docks had been constructed due to the insistent demands made by growing trade and the increasing size of ships. Prince of Wales Dock (No 5) followed in 1895, and Trafalgar Dock (No 6) in 1905. Patriotism was certainly the order of the day!

Above: The view through Gate No 8 at Southampton Docks, in January 1961, gives a tantalising glimpse of a mighty ship, but no doubt British Transport Commission security procedures would have prevented a casual stroll through for further investigation. Control over the docks has changed hands several times since their opening in 1838 by the Southampton, London & Branch Railway and Dock Company. By 1892, after much expansion, the entire docks undertaking had passed into the hands of the London and South Western Railway Company. Nationali-sation saw the docks pass under the control of the British Transport Commission in 1948, replaced by the British Transport Dock Board in 1963. The key change since then has been privatisation and the creation of Associated British Ports in 1982. The importance of the docks to Southampton can be measured by the fact that at this

Events of the 1960s

HOT OFF THE PRESS

Barbed wire, concrete blocks and a wide no-man's-land divided East from West when a reinforced wall was built right across the city of Berlin in 1961. Many East Germans escaped to the West at the eleventh hour, taking with them only the possessions they could carry. The Berlin Wall divided the city - and hundreds of family members and friends - for 28 years until the collapse of Communist rule across Eastern Europe. Who can ever forget those scenes in 1989, when ordinary people themselves began to physically tear down the hated wall?

THE WORLD AT LARGE

'One giant leap for mankind' was taken on 20th July 1969, when Neil Armstrong made history as the first man to set foot on the moon. During the mission he and fellow-astronaut 'Buzz' Aldrin collected rock and soil samples, conducted scientific experiments - and had a lot of fun jumping around in the one-sixth gravity. Twenty-one hours and thirty-seven minutes after their landing they took off again in their lunar module 'Eagle' to rejoin Apollo II which was orbiting above them, proudly leaving the American flag on the Moon's surface.

ROYAL WATCH

Princess Margaret's announcement in 1960 that she was to wed photographer Antony Armstrong-Jones (later Lord Snowdon) brought sighs of relief from her immediate family. Just five years earlier the people of Britain had sympathised as the princess bowed to public and private pressure, ending her relationship with Peter Townsend, Prince Philip's former equerry. The Church (and the Queen, as its Head) frowned on the liaison as Townsend was divorced. Her marriage to Lord Snowdon itself ended in 1978.

Docks are a fascinating mixture of the romantic and the mundane. The romance is associated with mighty liners, luxury cruises and the parade of the wealthy and famous. The mundane consists of the day-by-day handling of all manner of cargo, the work of dredgers and tugs, and the routine maintenance required. This shot of March 1963 certainly falls into the mundane category, even though the rather fine looking Falaise occupies some of the background.

Two or three barges are tied up at this inner dock, with plenty of work in progress. Everywhere there is evidence of commerce and activity - the ubiquitous dockside cranes, the warehouse, the stacked pallets and the smoking tug. Of course it was the prime purpose of dealing with trade rather than passengers that led to the creation of Southampton Docks in 1838, and shortly afterwards the Royal Mail Steam Packet Company based itself at Southampton, with a government contract to convey mails between Great Britain and the West Indies and the Americas. At the time of the photograph two of the major import items were wool and fruit, with over a quarter of a million bales of wool shipped through the port annually.

The age of the great passenger liners might well have reached its twilight by 1963, the date of this photograph, but they still make an impressive sight in the dusk of a floodlit Ocean Dock. On view from left to right are Queen Elizabeth, Franconia and Andes. Officially launched in 1938, Queen Elizabeth had the strangest of maiden voyages. Zig-zagging across the Atlantic to avoid U-boats, she joined her sister ship, Queen Mary, in New York. Both ships spent the rest of the war as troop carriers, mainly across the North Atlantic. After the war, her role as a passenger ship lasted only until 1968 when she was

Memories of SOUTHAMPTON

sold by Cunard. Ultimately she was destroyed by fire in Hong Kong, in 1972, on the verge of being converted into the floating Seawise University. More than one Cunarder has carried the name Franconia, and the one featured in the photograph was launched in 1954. She sailed between Southampton and Montreal for some years, and did a little cruising also. She was sold to Russia in 1973, and renamed Fedor Shalyapin. The 26,000 ton Andes acquired her fame both working for the Royal Mail Line on the South American service, and as a cruise liner, until she was withdrawn in 1971.

At work

This elevated view of the docks was captured at a time when the big liners were very much in evidence, before the rise of air travel began to have such an impact on passenger business. Lines of railway coaches can be seen in the middle distance, whilst the smoke of a docks shunter is visible in the centre of the photograph. Warehouses, sheds and cranes also help to create that special docks atmos-

phere of loading and unloading, arrivals and departures. The docks at Southampton have provided its citizens with many spectacles which in some ways have mirrored our commercial and military history. During the Crimean War (1854 - 1856) the P & O Company alone disembarked 90,000 men. These figures were eclipsed by the massive number of soldiers - over seven million - who passed

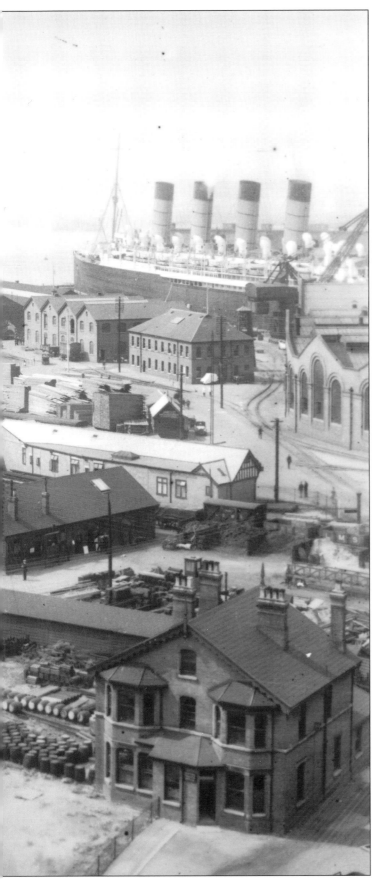

Events of the 1960s

MELODY MAKERS

The 1960s: those were the days when the talented blues guitarist Jimi Hendrix shot to rock stardom, a youthful Cliff Richard charmed the nation with his 'Congratulations' and Sandie Shaw won the Eurovision Song Contest for Britain with 'Puppet on a String'. It was the combined musical talents of a group of outrageous working-class Liverpool lads, however, who formed the Beatles and took the world by storm with music that ranged from the experimental to ballads such as 'Yesterday'.

INVENTION AND TECHNOLOGY

A major step forward was made in 1960 when the laser was invented. An acronym for Light Amplification by Stimulated Emission of Radiation, the device produces a narrow beam of light that can travel for vast distances and is focused to give enormous power. Laser beams, as well as being able to carry far more information than radio waves, can also be used for surgery, cutting, drilling, welding and scores of other operations.

SCIENCE AND DISCOVERY

When the drug Thalidomide was first developed during the 1950s it was hailed as a wonder drug which would ease the distressing symptoms of pregnancy sickness. By the early 1960s the drug's terrible side effects were being discovered, when more than 3000 babies had been born with severe birth defects. Malformed limbs, defective eyes and faulty intestines were the heart-rending legacy left by Thalidomide.

through the port during the first world war. Ships were sometimes leaving the docks at a rate of 25 to 30 per night between 1914 and 1918. The constant opening of new docks and dry docks reflected the rise of Britain's trade, and as these were often named after and opened by royalty, this provided more impressive occasions for Sotonians. Such were the attractions of the port that by 1939 around 500,000 sight-seers were arriving each year to see the great liners.

Above: Saturday, July 19th 1941, was the concluding day of War Weapons Week in Southampton, and this was earmarked as Civil Defence Day. A section of the Docks Air Raid Precaution and Fire Services are shown here, being marshalled at the dockside for their part in the day's proceedings. The vehicles look the part for 1941, and the fine old Capstan advertisement on the hoarding to the far left adds an extra touch of authenticity. Fighting the war was costing Britain an immense amount of money, and right across the country huge drives were held in order to persuade people to buy such things as government War Bonds and Defence Bonds. In addition towns and cities often adopted regiments, ships or air squadrons, supporting them in various ways. All this provided both material benefits and a feeling of national solidarity. War Weapons Week was one of such drives, and in Southampton's week the target was set at £750,000. The specific aim was enough money to buy two destroyers for the protection of merchant shipping, a very appropriate target for Southampton. A destroyer's mast was raised in the forecourt of the Civic Centre, and the honour of posting the running total on the mast fell to a different group daily.

Right: The honour for the final day of War Weapons Week fell to Civil Defence, and the close-up shows some of the men and vehicles that were doing such sterling work in fire-fighting and Air Raid Precaution at the docks, usually in the most dangerous of circumstances. The preceding week had seen a variety of events to arouse public interest and get the money rolling. The Mayor, Councillor W Lewis, opened proceedings in a ceremony on July 12th, and this was followed by a grand parade of the Forces, along with ex-servicemen's and women's organisations. A major event during the week was a cricket match between a Southampton XI (including two Hampshire players) and the Police. Other sporting activities included a tennis tournament, a tug-of-war contest and a physical training display by the Federation of Boys' Clubs. An unusual feature of the week was a model circus and working model fairground, created out of scrap metal by three Sotonians, and put on display at 122 Above Bar. The importance of such collective efforts to the government was shown by messages of support from Ernest Bevin, Minister of Labour, and the First Lord of the Admiralty. Both alluded to the courageous resistance of the citizens of Southampton to fierce enemy air attacks.

There are many reasons for using the services of divers in a docks area, but the date of this photograph, September 4th 1940, suggests that this particular exercise may have been connected with the war that was currently raging. The scene is the Inner Dock, and perhaps the diver is looking for bomb damage sustained below water level. While one man assists the diver with his line, the other one appears to be anxiously scanning the horizon. And well he might, for since August 13th 1940 German bombers had been regularly hitting the Old Docks and the riverside factories and shipyards along the Itchen. Woolston had been of particular interest to the bombers, with the presence there of Thornycroft's shipbuilding yards and the Spitfire producing Supermarine factory. The very first raid on the Old Docks, on August 13th, had seen a spectacular fire resulting from direct hits on the Cold Store at berths 40 and 41. The Cold Store had been opened in 1901, and with a capacity of 1,700,000 cubic feet, was the largest refrigerated cargo store in Europe. Fed by 2,345 tons of butter, the inferno could not be quenched in spite of the application of around 10,000,000 gallons of water, and it had to be left to burn itself out.

a lot of damage to what was now known as Southampton Central. A patching up operation took place until the station was totally rebuilt in 1967, with the loss of the clock tower. The photograph shows the rather dismal immediate post-war phase, with half-finished and temporary structures everywhere, albeit with some striking posters advertising OXO, Guinness and Daz.

Top: It's probably as well for them that none of Hitler's stormtroopers ever tried to invade Southampton, for these ladies would have given them short shrift. They were engaged in demolition work at the docks, no doubt dealing with structures made unsafe by German bombing, especially during 1940 and 1941. As well as joining auxiliary uniformed branches of all the armed services, women contributed to the war effort in a multitude of ways. As in the first great conflict, women had to fill the gap left by the demands of conscription on the male population. Women joined the Land Army, produced munitions and engaged in industrial work of every kind. For example, a former stewardess in a liner turned her hand to repairing army vehicles in Southampton, overhauling three engine a week. The voluntary organisations worked in the front line of Civil Defence, and women were to the fore here as ambulance drivers, air raid wardens and first-aid workers. The Women's Voluntary Service had been formed specifically in 1938 with the object of coping with the consequences of bombing on the civilian population. It did sterling work in this and in a host of other capacities. The women demolition workers on the truck were just a few of a mighty army.

Above: It is hard to credit now that this 1954 scene was a view of the area around the present day Southampton Central station - so much has changed. The commercial possibilities of railways were not lost on enterprising men, and Southampton was directly linked to London by rail in 1840. Southampton West station was opened in 1895 to replace the old Blechynden - West End station, and its most prominent feature was the rather splendid 100 feet high clock tower. The success and popularity of rail travel in this area is revealed by the fact that this station handled the second largest volume of passenger traffic on the London and South Western Railway after Waterloo. By 1934 to 1935 there was further expansion, this time under the Southern Railway. The number of platforms was increased to four and stylish new station buildings were created. Unfortunately World War II bombing did

From barrow boy to cash and carry supremo

I f ever there was a case of the self made man in business, then Alan Veal suits that description perfectly. Even so, never in his widest dreams could he have imagined how it would all turn out. Seeing that young chap in his 20s, back in the early 1950s, you could be forgiven for thinking that he was just another barrow boy trying to earn a modest living from the stall he had set up in the city centre. Well, really, that is exactly what he was. Like many others before him and since, his ambitions were to make his way in the world. That world as he first knew it was one of post-war rationing and austerity. Food was still in short supply and the Attlee

government was in its final days before good old Winnie returned to power. Alan would have been whistling the tunes of Guy Mitchell, Jimmy Young and the Stargazers as he loaded his barrow with whatever fruit and veg he could get from the wholesaler that day. Apples, pears and tomatoes were all keenly priced in figures that the young-sters of today would not recognise. Ninepence a pound or two bob for a big bagful are words that the young 'uns (that is anyone under 40!) would never have used. They were part and parcel of everyday language to young Alan as he tried to encourage the housewife to open her tight purse. Part of the ritual was the friendly banter that took place between them. 'How's the old man today, love?' was

a good opener to get the customer moaning on about 'him indoors'. Then a quick recommendation of the quality and value of the goods he had on sale, along with 'half a pound of juicy Cox's pippins will soon put some spice back into your life', and the transaction was complete. While she was hooked, the housewife could always be encouraged to pick up couple of pears for the kids. It was a routine they would repeat regularly. A good customer and proprietor relationship was a firm basis for a successful business, however small in its beginnings. Alan and his customers recognised the need for the friendly chat in building a bond that would guarantee satisfaction on both sides. The customer accepted that she was valued

and came to rely on him for both a pleasant shopping experience and an economical one. He was happy to build a firm client base. Who knows? Perhaps there might be a banana or two on the stall to-morrow. You could always dream. If there was, Alan might keep one back just for her, or so the shopper might think.

It is that sort of interest in the needs of the individual that has helped AR Veal Ltd become the multi million pound business it is to-day. Whilst being a mammoth enterprise these days, Veal's has not lost the plot. The customer is still the focus of attention. The Veal family has recognised that the sort of mutual confidence that existed in those days of the barrow can be and must be transferred to the larger scene. To see the business today is to see how successful the Veals have been in keeping their priorities right. No sleeping partners in this firm or pie in the sky thinking. It is very much a down to earth and practical way of running a busy company. Alan's three sons have now taken over the running of AR Veal Ltd, but it still keeps faith with the way in which he established it. These three directors acknowledge the business ethic taught them by their father and have carried the firm forward into the new millennium with a mixture of pride in achievement and further ambition for the years that lie ahead.

Left: *How it all began...Alan Veal with his barrow in 1951.*

Above: The rented warehouse which the company occupied between 1966 and 1988. It was bought in 1976 and is now the company's carpark.

But Alan would be the first to admit that it was not a complete one man band. Behind every successful businessman there stands a good woman, so they say. They did not come much better than Heather. Alan's wife and mother to the three lads was a tower of strength, especially in those days of struggling against the competition of other traders and the 'big boys' in the business. As well as running the family home, she was at Alan's side whenever another pair of hands was needed. If ever there were dark days, and there were some, she was able to provide the support and encouragement that spurred him on. He had come from humble beginnings and knew the value of hard work, but it was always good to have someone to work with and for. Heather and the boys provided that target.

Alan Veal had begun his working life as a cowman. Having spent two years as a National Serviceman, he started his fruit and veg business from the barrow shortly after

> *After a while, it was obvious to him that he needed to change his style of business*

completing his time in the forces. The sense of discipline that National Service gave to young men helped him devote his efforts into succeeding as a trader. He also had an eye for an opportunity and would buy and sell virtually any commodity that would yield a profit. Working from home and at the markets he soon built up a flourishing and regular trade. In the 1950s a typical week would see him starting off at Fareham Market on a Monday. The following day, he would move on to Alton Market. Here he would set up his stall by 7 am and work until 6 pm. If that was not enough, the day had hardly begun for this workaholic. Alan left Alton to take his lorry to Southampton for the sea crossing to Le Havre. When the ferry berthed at dawn on the Wednesday, he was then off to the Arcoroc factory near the Belgium border. Here he loaded up with glass and china and whizzed back along the French highways to catch the 10 o'clock night sailing back home. There was no time to rest on his laurels, because it was straight off to London to sell on his cargo to the wholesaler. Then he could go back home for a well earned rest before the whole process began again. At least he did not do what one driver managed during the miners' strike of the 70s. He collected the 20 tons of candles in France which Alan had purchased, drove to Le Havre docks, missed the bridge and landed in the water. The driver ended up in hospital and they are still fishing candles out of the harbour to this day!

However, a market trader can only go so far. After a while, it was obvious to him that he needed to change his style of business and find premises that offered greater opportunity for expansion. AR Veal moved to Netley Abbey, where it stayed for the next 10 years. When greater expansion was needed, the search was on for something that would enable the business to sell a wide range of merchandise at discount prices. the larger the stock that could be carried, then the greater the discounts that could be negotiated. At last, a warehouse on the Portsmouth road at Sholing was identified. It was a large, empty building that seemed ideal. As a brand new building it was in need of decoration. The Veal family pooled their resources and held a painting

party. It was all shoulders to the wheel and the family came up trumps. The painting of the warehouse was finished in just one weekend. Some members of the family were heard to remark that they wished the same effort could be put into painting the window frames at home, but it was treated with good humour. It was still a difficult job to raise enough money to fit out the building and buy stock. Added to this, there were four markets per week to be worked. An 18 hour day was the norm rather than the exception; a pattern that continued for many years. Success does not come without sweat and Alan Veal and his family shed bucket loads.

The Sholing warehouse was bought by the family in 1976, having rented it for a decade. Eight years later, following plans to expand again, a new warehouse, costing £1.5 million, was begun across the road. The bank had been so impressed with the outline of the venture that it agreed to loan the company £1 million towards the development. The old warehouse was demolished and the site is now AR Veal's customer car park. Keen buying and keeping the profit margin low have helped keep the Veal business one step ahead of its competitors. The threat of the superstores and take-over bids is always there, but an eye for detail, an excellent reputation and competitive pricing has seen AR Veal continue to be the region's largest family owned retail cash and carry outlet, serving the local public in both the wholesale and retail trade.

Left: *The Veal family. From left to right: Paul, Stephen, Heather, Alan and Mark.*
Below: *The current premises which are sited next to the old warehouse. The Veal family did most of the work on the new building.*

All hands on deck as the cars go to ground

It is a fact of life that we will spend more money buying cars over the years than our house cost us. We spend a huge amount of our money and a lot of our time in simply maintaining and looking after them, as well as driving them around from A to B. Insurance premiums are high, repair costs massive and the price of petrol just seems to go up and up and up. Yet, we cannot manage without them. Successive governments will try to tell us to get on public transport and to help the environment by pulling the old pushbike from the shed. Whilst draughty buses and trains do not run to time or serve the routes we want, the motor car will continue to reign supreme. It is no longer a luxury; it is a necessity. Even when we go away on holiday or off on a business trip without it, the car is still a consideration. Imagine that you are going on a cruise from Southampton. What do you do with the old jalopy? Everyone knows you are away, so it is vulnerable in the garage or out on the street. All tearaway teenagers seem to know how to hot-wire, so that is not a safe solution. It could be left with the 19 year old son. Perish the thought! You want to return to a car

that has been carefully looked after, not blazed up and down the M3 at 100 mph. In any case, you need to get suitcases and baggage, as well as your husband, down to the docks. Taxis are expensive and sometimes

Below: The Docks premises in the 1920s.
Bottom: The company's original premises in High Street.

unreliable. Anyway, they would not solve the problem of what to do with the family motor. The answer is waiting for you, down at dockside.

Andrews (Shipside Services) Limited is waiting to provide the solution. Away with you to the Mediterranean, or wherever it is you are about to be whisked off to, and leave the professionals to handle the problem that has been furrowing your brow for so long. Andrews provides a shipside car service that lets you sleep easily, knowing that 'Genevieve' is in safe hands. The premises, based at both the Eastern and Western docks, are completely within the perimeter of the Docks Estate. All you need to do is drive up to the departure berth and hand over your luggage to one of the porters who will take it ready for loading aboard. That is when Andrews Ltd takes over. A company representative takes over

control of the car and all you have to do is inform him of what you need. Any cleaning, servicing or repairs will be carried out, just as you wish. If you forgot to top up the tank before arriving in the port, just tell Andrews and you will find on your return that the petrol has been supplied. Your car is driven away by a fully qualified and insured driver and taken to a secure compound where it will stay under lock and key all the time you are away. There is room in the under-cover area and compound for over 1,500 cars. A back-up fleet of personnel carriers and service vans are always on hand to provide extra assistance. There are even arrangements that can be made for collection and delivery at airports when people are undertaking 'fly-cruises'. So,

Above: *A Hutmobile pulling a fuel bowser in the 1930s.*

driving down from Birmingham or flying in from Manchester, means that there is one less matter on your mind. Andrews has been connected with Southampton Docks since 1920, so it is hardly surprising that the company does a good job. It has had years of practice!

The business can be traced back through two generations of Stubbs and five of the Andrews family to the early 19th century. Originally known as Andrews Bros, it was started by Richard Andrews in 1832. A blacksmith's son, he was a former wheelwright who had been apprenticed to a firm of coach builders in Bishops Sutton, near Winchester. As a young man in his early 20s, Richard moved to Southampton and began work servicing and repairing the various types of coaches and carriages that visited the many coaching inns around the town centre. He soon began to move into coach building for himself and achieved early fame as a skilful worker. So well did he do that he exhibited at

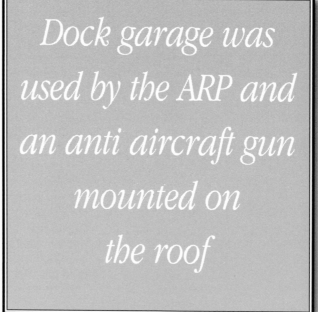

Dock garage was used by the ARP and an anti aircraft gun mounted on the roof

the Great Exhibition of 1851 and received the Royal Warrant from Queen Victoria. The pony carriage that she used later in life is kept at Osborne House, on the Isle of Wight. It was built by Andrews. His fame was not limited to the carriage industry. Mr Andrews was Mayor of Southampton on five occasions. His son and grandson carried on the business after Richard had died. By the time the first world war came along, the work had moved into the area of motor body building and general garaging services. During that war, a fleet of London taxis was serviced at Andrews and then shipped over the Channel to act as transport reinforcements for the soldiers in retreat from Mons. A great many ambulances were built, including one that was the first to have a swing down top stretcher, and any number of

Below: This picture dates from the 1960s and shows Andrews servicing the Queen Elizabeth. The company services the present QE2 which still carries cars.

makers were travelling to the Channel Islands, taking day trips to France and going cruising. The cruise car garage service was born. This developed under the guidance of Jack Andrews, the great grandson of the founder. He piloted its successful growth until his retirement in 1963. During that time a transport department was developed. It was later taken over by British Road Services. New premises within the docks were opened and a service station built. A steam cleaning system was established in 1956 when the Americans demanded that all cars entering the country were free from contamination and, therefore, mud free. 'Trust them,' thought Jack, but he turned it to the company's advantage. The system is approved and officially recognised throughout the world. Nowadays, Andrews also has one of only two US approved Plumbtesto test stations in this country. A car hire department was begun in 1954 and the company was sold to the Hertz organisation four years later, whilst keeping the family name.

Frederick Stubbs became the MD in 1971. He was in charge when the Stubbs family bought the company in 1979. Frederick's son, Roderick, became managing director in 1985. By virtue of its own good practices, the company has seen off most of its competitors. By providing a trusted service with a high level of security, it has generated a huge amount of repeat business. That, alone, is an excellent recommendation. It also shares the respect of the cruise companies and port operators. An experienced staff is well known to port personnel and that helps provide a shared motive in meeting the passengers' particular requirements in an efficient way. Most people in Southampton seem to have worked here at some time or other. Pictures or features about the company are forever popping up in museums and magazines. Everyone seems to know about Andrews. Why not? It provides a unique service.

Army transport vehicles were serviced. In the war that followed the Eastern Dock garage was used by the ARP and an anti-aircraft gun mounted on the roof.

After nearly a century at its site on High Street, the Andrews company moved to Southampton Docks in 1920 and has stayed there, although at different premises, ever since. As the world was opening up, thanks to the greater distances covered and speeds attained by the modern liners of the day, Andrews Bros saw an opportunity for a near unique development. People were being more adventurous in their travel arrangements and the well-to-do middle and upper classes had taken to the motor car in a big way. Spotting a gap in the market is often the formula for success. This is exactly what happened to Andrews. The dockside service was born. Established in what can only be described a tin hut with space for half a dozen cars, petrol was sold in the standard two gallon cans. This was in the days before petrol pumps. Wooden packing cases were made for the storage of cars that were to be carried on sea voyages. At that time, cars were regarded as freight. The business grew to include local haulage and baggage delivery and collection. By around 1930, the main pattern of today's business emerged. Holiday-

Above: 10 Gate Garage in the 1960s.
Top: Jack Andrews in 1960.
Right: The company's present managing director Rod Stubbs and operations director Sharon Butler.

A spoonful of sugar helps the medicine ....

Sugaring the pill is an expression that came into the English language during the 19th century. Like many of our sayings, it has an origin that can be traced to a particular event or an occasion. For this one we can thank the American, William R Warner. In his Philadelphia drugstore he developed and sold the first sugar coated pills that were to set the scene for making nasty medicines and tablets acceptable to the palate. No longer would it be the case that if medication tastes bad then it must be doing you good. Warner joined forces with another innovative pharmacist, Jordan W Lambert. He had concocted an antiseptic solution that he named Listerine, no doubt in homage to the pioneer of research into the field of

antiseptics. So it was that the Warner-Lambert company began. Today its name is associated with an ability to develop superior products that have become household names across the globe. A truly international concern, Warner-Lambert sells its pharmaceuticals, consumer health care and confectionery products in 150 countries and has 78 production plants dotted across the world. In Britain the pharmaceutical products are marketed by Parke-Davis.

The roots of Parke-Davis lie in America. In the 1860s Sam Duffield, a

Above: A spread from the 1903 catalogue.
Below: Some of the company's earliest products.

doctor and chemist, tried his hand in business. He opened a drugstore and tinkered with developing his own brands of medicines and potions. His inventions included Ether, Sweet Spirit of Nitre and Oil of Wine. However, although he was a gifted scientist, his business know-how left a lot to be desired. Enter Hervey C Parke. He had just made a healthy profit from selling a mining hardware business and was looking for another investment. Joining forces with Duffield in 1866, they became Duffield, Parke & Company. Straight away they went into production, but needed someone to go on the road to promote their wares. The young George Davis, was taken on. He already had a reputation as a high power salesman and he was the prime mover behind the first advertising brochure the company produced. It was typical of the age. All manner of glowing testimonials covered its pages, highly recommending the strength and benefits of Duffield's Medicinal Fluid Extracts. The extracts were from such wonderful sources as angelica, balsam, juniper, liquorice, liverwort and so on; the list was seemingly endless. The product bore the famous

> *The foundations for the company's international success were laid in this period of the late 19th century*

trademark, 'Medicamenta', meaning 'truth in medicine'. Although Duffield did not stay long with the company, Parke and Davis went along in leaps and bounds. From 1871, the company bore their names. The foundations for the company's international success were laid in this period of the late 19th century. Over the next 100 years it would rise to become America's 14th largest pharmaceutical manufacturer, until it became part of the massive Warner-Lambert business in 1970.

The first overseas branch of Parke-Davis first appeared in Britain in 1891. An outlet was opened on Holborn Viaduct in London, not far from St Paul's Cathedral. Two American brothers, Fred and Harry Fisk, were the managers. Fred died in 1915 and Harry continued to oversee the London office and the European expansion until his death in 1927. By then, the term 'Europe' had become very flexible. The London office controlled events in Madagascar, the Middle East, Angola, Russia and a number of other countries that would hardly

Above: *The Parke-Davis premises in the 1960s.*

countries that would hardly regard themselves as ever considering to apply for membership of the EEC. Some of them stayed under the wing of London until the 50s and 60s. The growth owed a lot to the Fisk brothers. Recognising that a huge and largely untapped market existed outside the States, they arranged for the distribution of Parke-Davis medical literature in Chinese, Japanese, Urdu, Gujerati, Arabic and Sinhalese as well as the obvious European languages. The Parke-Davis catalogue of this era was some 250 pages in length, a sure reflection of the distance the company had come in less than 30 years in business. Exotic preparations vied with the traditional. There was Wild Ginger or Wild Indigo to be had. For six shillings, a steep price in Victorian England, you could take the fluid extract of Wild Lettuce. Iron and quinine tablets were popular and morphine sulphate was available at 2/10d (14p) for a bottle of 500. One of the most popular products of the day was Euthymol toothpaste. It is probably the world's oldest branded toothpaste and is still going strong a century later. Although the general public got to know the company through the success of products like this, Parke-Davis was anxious to get itself well known by doctors and pharmacists. The quality of the products and the reliability they offered soon convinced the medical world that here was a company to be trusted. The development of pepsin in the late 1880s, desiccated thyroid gland in the 1890s and the introduction of adrenaline, the first hormone to be isolated in pure form, in 1901 all added to the reputation of the company. It was a time of revolution in the medical field. Antitoxins and vaccines against diphtheria, influenza, streptococcus and typhoid made it an exciting time to be involved. Parke-Davis was at the cutting edge. Manufacture and research was begun on a new site in Hounslow and other offices were opened on Queen Victoria Street and at Beak Street. These latter offices were the UK headquarters until 1947.

In the 1920s the company led the field in the research and development of vitamins. Not everything is down to systematic study, observation and painstaking trialling. Every so often, lady luck plays her hand. During this time, a large bird was discovered in the laboratory. Whether it was exhausted by its efforts to escape or had been struck down with some ailment, no-one was really sure. However, some bright spark decided to give the creature a dose of an experimental vitamin preparation. To everyone's surprise, with the exception of the chap who had the brainwave, the bird made an energetic recovery. With much flapping of wings and loud squawking it took off through an open door and out into the blue yonder. To show its appreciation it kindly left no sign of its passing overhead on the cars in the car park underneath! By the 1950s, Hounslow had produced hundreds of new products and preparations. Perhaps one of the most important of this post-war period was Chloromycetin, the first antibiotic to be an effective treatment for typhoid. It was also effective against whooping cough, meningeal infection and pneumonia. The general public will instantly recognise one particular product from this period. It is Benylin. Every tickle in the throat or chesty cough has at one time or another had the Benylin soothing treatment.

Above: *The company's Eastleigh premises today.*

As the 60s stopped swinging, Parke-Davis was experiencing some difficulties. There were few new products being developed and its competitors were becoming increasingly bullish in their production and marketing. The company still retained a major trump card. The very name of Parke-Davis still had a ring of reliability in

quality, service and expertise about it. The time was ripe for Warner-Lambert to take control. As part of the modernisation plans for Parke-Davis, relocation of the Hounslow operation to Pontypool, South Wales, was determined. The job of integrating the company with Warner-Lambert in the 1970s fell to the late JT Beasley. He arranged for the administration of Parke-Davis to be relocated again, this time to Eastleigh. At first, the name that had been a byword in the medical profession and in the minds of the general public was gradually sidelined. Sales did not respond well. By the mid 1980s, Alan Walker, at that time General Sales Manager had taken a hand. His own experience in sales convinced him that a strong sense of purpose and a high profile was what Parke-Davis needed. He relaunched the UK Pharmaceutical Division as Parke-Davis Research Laboratories (PDRL). A new range of products, such as Erymax and Mucolex, were introduced. The company began to head forward again. A neuroscience research centre was established at Cambridge and, from its base in Eastleigh, Parke-Davis can again advance with a skilled and motivated workforce providing the engine to the management's drive. As its mission statement says, 'This is a caring company and a source of pride for all who work in it'.

Left: Hector Graham, Regional President (1983-1988) and Alan Walker. *Below:* Alan Walker, current Regional President of Parke-Davis British Isles and Nordic.

Still delivering the goods, a century later

Great oak trees from little acorns grow. The famous saying sums up many of the large businesses that flourish in and around our cities. Everything has to make a start somewhere; after all, success and growth do not arrive overnight. What started as a small corner shop in the Freemantle district of Southampton over 103 years ago is today Sibley Material Movements Limited, a busy haulage operation covering a large area of the South of England with a fleet of tipper lorries.

Thomas Sibley had been a tool maker, working in the docks. It was there that he received a nasty injury that proved to be a blessing in disguise. It was the compensation money that helped him to set up in business for himself. He made that move into the commercial sector when he and his wife Rose took charge of a shop on Park Road in Freemantle. Here they set up the general grocery, corn and coal merchant's business. His son, William (WT Sibley)

and sister Lily both worked in the shop. It was already a true family business. It was hard work, and Tom would make his son William go out before he went to school on a delivery round, taking anything from coke and coal, to corn, fruit and vegetables. This invariably made him late for school and he would get the cane from the school master. Alice Wheeler knew William, and also knew why he was late and felt sorry for him. Their friendship grew

Above left: William T Sibley, founder of the company.
Below: William T Sibley, aged 12.
Bottom: Tom and Rose Sibley with William and Lily c1905, Cawte Road, Freemantle.

Five years later the first Ford commercial vehicle was purchased. People think that the model T Ford was just a saloon, but there were lorries as well. The one the Sibleys bought was a one ton truck, and as business flourished between the wars it was the first in a long line of Ford vehicles. One major project during this period was the Sibley involvement in the building of the civic centre - an undertaking which was a source of great family pride. By the outbreak of World War II the fleet of

from school days and they married in 1915. William decided upon returning from the First World War to buy out his father with an annuity. Alice had some private funds and helped William to achieve this. In 1919 William Thomas took over the running of the business. He had great vision and conducted his business in an honourable fashion. In 1923 new premises were found at Shirley Road and trade was expanded, developing the haulage side of the business, purchasing land, working sand and gravel pits. Also land and property were purchased for rental.

Fords numbered 18 and other premises had been bought, including a yard at Millbrook Road. The family company had officially become WT Sibley (Haulage) Ltd in 1935. Alice's brother, Gus, was the Company Secretary and they did all the book work together. Other in-laws and family members joined the business, over the years. WT Sibley's sons, William Jr and Ronald, became involved either side of the war, though the elder son spent most of the

Above left: *Ben Loft with his Ford B.B.*
Top: *The fleet of lorries in the mid 1930s.*

war serving his country in the Maritime Royal Artillery. During the war years the firm was heavily involved in the supply of building materials, fulfilling war contracts. One of the unfortunate growth areas in the war came as a result of enemy activity. There was always debris to be cleared and removed after a raid. In peacetime, the company continued to build on the reputation it had gained for reliability in carrying out its contracts in a professional manner. Sadly, WT died in 1952. He was only 58 years of age, but had achieved a great deal in establishing the haulage business as a major player in the city's commercial sector.

The company motto 'We deliver the goods' had been coined by WT, and his family continued to live up to the message after he had gone. Control passed into the hands of his widow and their four children, as there were also two girls, Rose (the eldest) and Phyllis. However, death duties provided the Sibleys with a major headache. Just when that cloud looked like being a stumbling block to further success, the sun and the gods smiled once more. They landed a major contract with Foster Wheeler and the fortunes were turned round. In fact, so remarkable was the change that the accountants had to double check

their figures as, at first, they were unable to accept that it was possible. But, they should have known the Sibleys better. There was no mistake and the future looked rosy once more. By this time the Millbrook yard had been sold and the business moved back to Dyer Road. During the 1960s other businesses were purchased as the company went from strength to strength. W Earl, HW Blow, Vacc's, Collins' of Winterslow and Shepherd's of Romsey all came under Sibley control.

Below: *From left to right: Joe Beauchamp, Len Davis, Frank Blow, Harry Combes, Ron Sibley.* **Bottom:** *The Sibley fleet in 1959 at Mayflower Park.*

Then in the 70s difficult times were again encountered with the fuel crisis and the three day week, also the death of Alice Sibley and her daughter Phyllis. In 1978 William's son Ron, the man chiefly responsible for taking all this heritage and expertise

Top: Part of today's fleet and workshop at Andes Road.
Above: A past Accountant, Colin Kosten's 70th birthday celebration with current managing director, John Sibley.
Right: Ron Sibley.

and turning it into a modern business, bought out his brother Bill and began running the business under the trade name of Material Movements with its distinctive lettering. Ron's son, John, joined at the same time, taking the family involvement into a fourth generation. In 1980, a particularly busy year for the company, Ron bought out the rest of the family and renamed the firm Sibley Material Movements Limited. He continued to develop and expand the company into Self Drive Hire and restarted the Tidy Bin business. He also renewed the whole fleet of vehicles in 1988. The Edbro Agency was acquired in the early 1990s and this is one of the currently expanding activities, along with the repair and maintenance of third party vehicles and the re-emergence of the Self Drive Hire trade. Sibleys is a company that values its employees as well as its clients. Long service by past trusted men such as Joe Beauchamp, George Finch and Colin Kosten, and presently by Ivor Tomlinson, shows that the workforce values the company as well.

Ron Sibley retired in 1997 after 45 years' service. He left confident in the knowledge that clients like Foster Yeoman, UMA Ltd, Tarmac Group, Hanson Aggregates and many, many more would continue to be well served by his son. John Sibley continues the family line, stretching back to great grandfather Tom.

Look all around and you know who built it

Portswood House Ltd stands impressively on its Millbrook site. It has been known as this since 1994 when Brazier & Son Holdings was renamed. The building contracting part of the business was sold in 1996 and later acquired by Kier, an international organisation that has offices at Portswood House. The Brazier name lives on as Brazier Construction under the Kier brand, as can be seen on hoardings up and down the region, and also as Brazier Interior Systems Limited, an independent company specialising in office interiors.

Locals still refer to anything to do with the company as Brazier's, because the family firm has been around in the construction and building industry for longer than anyone can remember.

It was as long ago as 1799 when the son of a carpet weaver, Charles Brazier, decided to branch out from the trade that had served his father well. Whilst revolution was in the air in France and heads were tumbling into baskets under the guillotine, Charles set his own minor rebellion into action. He served his time as an apprentice plumber and glazier before going it alone at Wilton. Having established himself as the first in a long line of Braziers that would continue through seven generations, he retired from the business quite early on. The reins were handed over to his son, another Charles, who was able to call on the services of three brothers, who were a carpenter, builder and painter. With various sectors of the building trade covered in their skills,

Right: The company's premises at 39-41 London Road during the King George V Coronation celebrations in 1911. Below: One of the company's earlier contracts.

the foundations of a successful family business were laid. The original offices of Charles Brazier still stand on North Street in Wilton. What changes they will have seen as the company has moved into its third century in the business. One of the reasons it has flourished can be linked to the attitude of its founder. He was not afraid to strike out into new territory and that has been the approach that has held the Braziers in good stead as the years have rolled by. The great changes, as Britain moved from an agricultural society to an industrial one, have been taken on by a firm that acknowledged that adaptation and flexibility were essential to development and prosperity. It is a fine balance between maintaining family traditions and not being stuck in the outmoded past. It is a balance that Brazier's has achieved with more than a degree of success.

In the 1840s, Daniel Brazier, who was the founder's grandson, came to Southampton. He worked in plumbing

all erected by the firm as business boomed. During the second world war, a decision was made to relocate to Portswood, and as plans were going ahead, the company's Above Bar and London Road premises were both destroyed by enemy action, bringing forward the move. After World War II, the company continued to have a major influence on the Southampton skyline. As well as work for the National Dock Labour Board, Brazier's was heavily involved with Southampton Council. Much of the remodelling of the town centre in the 1950s was this company's work.

In more modern times with Walter's son, Dudley Brazier, in principal role, Brazier's developed with a number of subsidiaries, including joinery, mechanical and electrical work, flooring, office interiors and general property development.

The family's involvement also expanded over this period when the seventh generation, Philip, Richard and Jonathan, joined the business.

Wherever you look, be it Poole's Arndale Centre, the Royal South Hants Hospital or that group of housing round the corner, then Brazier's probably built it.

Top: *The vehicle fleet in the mid 1930s.*
Above left: *An early advertisement.*
Below: *The head office in the 1960s.*

and glazing with a firm owned by Samuel Ingram. On his death, in 1859, Daniel took over the business. The family prospered in these late Victorian times. Brazier's was known as a large employer of labour and Daniel and son Charles as active and successful businessmen. Charles was busy in local church circles and politics. He moved to a large villa on Portswood Road, but tragically died of sunstroke a few years later. After his death, the firm became simply Brazier & Son.

Expansion was the name of the game in the 20th century. Early expenses for stabling soon disappeared as the business modernised and spread its net wider than plumbing and glazing. The Redcote brickworks at Bitterne were purchased. Brazier's could make its own bricks and the contracting and jobbing building work grew. It became a limited company in 1916 and the following year Walter Brazier, then Governing Director, became the President of Southampton and District Association of Building Trades Employers. The company was now firmly established as a major force in local commerce. Bowman's sawmill, blacksmith's and undertakers was taken over, though the latter two trades did not feature long in Brazier's plans! The first large contract in Corporation housebuilding was won and 52 houses built as Southampton tried to fulfil the national pledge of building homes fit for heroes from the Great War.

Between the wars, Brazier's was operating from four different sites including London Road and Above Bar. Cinemas, pubs, garages, libraries, schools and offices were

One hundred years in the driving seat

The year 1998 marked an impressive 100 years in the motor trade for the Hendy family business - and even before that, the family had already kept a couple of generations of Southampton folk on the road. Frederick Adolphus Hendy came to live and work in East Street, Southampton, in 1859, moving with his wife and five children from Whitchurch, where he had had a shop specialising in selling Falcon bicycles and outdoor clothing. Like most cycles dealers of the day, Frederick sold his own branded bicycles, assembled in his own shop from pre-manufactured components. In Southampton he was able to set up a larger works and the business expanded, becoming a fully limited company in 1898. Then Frederick diversified into four-wheeled transport, taking on agencies for Benz and Bolle. This was a rather unusual step for a bicycle dealer to take; as a general rule it was the blacksmiths and carriagebuilders traditionally involved in supplying horse-drawn carriages who progressed into selling motor cars. Nonetheless, Frederick Hendy launched himself into the business and began selling cars all over the UK; and in the process he became the owner of one of the first Benz horizontally opposed two-cylinder cars, which has remained a prized family possession ever since.

The business subsequently passed to Frederick's son Percy. Percy's approach was as bold as his father's had been: in 1910, with the Ford Motor Company of Great Britain preparing to repeat in Britain the tremendous success which its Model T already enjoyed in America, Percy Hendy signed an agreement with Henry Ford himself which made the Hendy Group the first official Ford Main Dealer in Great Britain.

The Model T, or 'Tin Lizzie', lived up to Ford's - and Percy's - expectations. Hendy's also dealt in Ford commercial vehicles, and between 1910 and 1914 the company grew rapidly, establishing outlets in Bournemouth and Southsea, while Percy also took part in rallies in the Model T. The outbreak of war then brought a change of direction and Hendy's became responsible for the maintenance and servicing of the Fordson tractors, vital to the nation's food production. When peace was restored, so was the popularity of the Model T; although the price had risen from £115 before the war to £220, it still accounted for 40 per cent of all new car sales.

Above left: Frederick Hendy, the founder.
Above right: Percy Hendy and his Model T Racer circa 1910. Below: The East Street Works circa 1900.

By the second world war Ford had moved to Dagenham and its range had expanded with introduction of the larger V8 engine, the smaller 8hp Y Type, and the Model A which was the Model T's replacement. Hendy's at Southampton, meanwhile, had moved first to Empress Road and then to Pound Tree Road where it established its headquarters and a motorcycle and accessory showroom; it also had premises in Vincent's Walk, a tractor sales department at Palmerston Road, and a bicycle retail and wholesale venture by the name of Accessories (Southampton) Limited in Brunswick Place; and the Chandlers Ford site had been opened in Bournemouth Road. During the war years Palmerston Road continued with truck and car servicing and also acted as a Ministry of Supply Auxiliary Workshop; meanwhile Vincent's Walk and Chandlers Ford were requisitioned by the Ministry of Aircraft Production and used as Spitfire factories when Supermarine's factory in Northam was bombed. The Pound Tree Road building was unfortunately destroyed in an air raid.

The war ended in 1945, but this time it was a number of years before trading conditions in the motor business returned to normal. The launch of the new Consul and Zephyr Six at the 1950 Earls Court Motor Show marked the beginnings of a new Ford range, and these two successful models were joined by the Anglia and Prefect in 1953. By the time of Hendy's 50th anniversary in 1959 the Group was also operating as Gordon Motors in Cosham, near Portsmouth, and had extended both its Chandlers Ford and its Vincent Walk premises; the company had passed into the hands of Percy's nephew Arthur Hendy following Percy's death in 1956.

The company had grown tremendously in its first 50 years, but was to grow even more in the next 50. Hendy Ford today is established as a leading car dealership throughout the region, while a separate organisation, Hendy Lennox

Commercial Vehicles Limited, has been set up to concentrate on the sale and servicing of Iveco Ford trucks. The Group also acts as a Honda agent, and other activities include vehicle leasing through Hendy Hire; the development and sales of the Gentrac Road Train and other specialist vehicles through Hendy Leisure Limited; and of course a very high-profile involvement in rallying through Hendy Motorsport, with Stephen Hendy himself, son of the current Chairman Norman V Hendy - and great great grandson of the founder F A Hendy - enjoying considerable success in the Escort Cosworth. The tradition of success is strong within the Hendy Group; the company has proved time and time again that it is quick to recognise a good opportunity and flexible enough to adapt; so although it is impossible to predict exactly what the next 100 or even 50 years will bring, there can be no doubt at all that much will happen and that the Hendy Group has a bright future ahead of it.

Above: *Southampton Carnival 1959.*
Below: *The Shirley Road premises acquired in 1998.*

No problem is beyond the WIT of Ashurst Lodge

To understand the unique contribution which Wessex Institute of Technology, at Ashurst Lodge, makes to industry across the globe, it is necessary to be aware of three things: that the work of Wessex Institute is focused on BEM; that BEM stands for boundary element method, and that the boundary element method is a computational method of solving engineering problems. And to fully appreciate the importance of its contribution, it is also necessary to be aware that - small though it is with an academic staff of ten working alongside 25 postgraduate research students - WIT is a pioneer in its field and is regarded by many as a blueprint for academia-industry collaboration.

The man behind WIT is Professor Carlos Brebbia. Born in Argentina, Carlos Brebbia obtained a PhD in civil engineering at Southampton University in 1968, and went on to pursue a successful academic career. His interest lay in developing the application of computational techniques to engineering practice - this was a time when mathematics and computers were just beginning to become an important part of engineering - and in 1980 Professor Brebbia gave up his post at the University of California at Irvine to return to Southampton, and set up the Computational Mechanics Institute. The commercial success of this project enabled the founding of the Wessex Institute of Technology in 1986.

Because WIT operates outside the university environment, it can make industry its first priority. Research is carried out in collaboration with commercial partners, and many postgraduate students come from industry. WIT has worked with dozens of blue chip companies including British Aerospace, Rolls Royce and United Technology Group; it has customers in this country, America, Japan, and virtually every industrialised nation of the world. It has worked on topics from the modelling of corrosion in ships to cracking in aerospace materials. It offers short courses; it organises conferences; it has an associated publishing company which brings out some 60 titles a years; it has developed its own software, including a package called BEASY which is becoming increasingly widely used within the engineering community, and it offers full support to all its software users. In short, it is an academic research institution which is fully committed to industry, and as such is one of a kind.

Above left: *Carlos Brebbia, founder of the Institute.*
Below: *Ashurst Lodge, the Institute's home.*

From farrier to Formula I, that's the 20th century for you

It is that rich mix of tradition and technology that has helped F Musson & Son Ltd keep a position in engineering that has earned the respect of other local companies. They know that if a problem is brought to Musson's, the know how and experience exists to design and build the machinery to solve it. Although the company is still evolving in the field of technology, as this area seems to go ahead by leaps and bounds on a daily basis, there is one sphere in which there is no change. In fact, it is not even an area for discussion, never mind, compromise. Throughout the 100 years or more that Musson's has been in business, quality and a pride in the job in hand have been the most important features of the company's success. These values have been firmly kept to by the three generations of the Musson family that have been involved in the running of the business.

Fredrick Musson founded the company in 1888. He had served an apprenticeship as a blacksmith and farrier and started on his own at Tangley near Andover. He moved to the present site in Shirley in 1900. There the business developed, working for many of the large estates which existed on the outskirts of Southampton.

It was the way of things then for sons to follow their fathers and the business passed to his son Herbert who was a true master craftsman and under his guidance the shoeing work was discontinued as the trade shrank with the spread of car ownership. Iron work for the many local building companies provided much of the trade at that time.

During World War II much work was carried out for the aircraft industry and the Royal Engineers as part of the war effort.

Today, under the directorship of Ian Musson, grandson of the founder, the company continues to meet the demands of the modern world and has moved into more specialised engineering work such as the design and manufacture of special purpose machines and of hydraulic equipment for the telecommunications industry and for Formula I engineering teams.

Top left: *Frederick Musson, the founder.*
Above: *The old blacksmith's shop in Shirley.*
Below: *The present day premises on the same site.*

A diver being assisted into the Inner Dock in a scene from September 1940.

Acknowledgments

The publishers are grateful for the assistance given by several local people and organisations which made the publication of this book possible:
Stephen Grace of Southampton City Libraries, and his colleague David Hollingworth, allowed access to the extensive collection of images held in the Special Collections department of the Central Library and also proved invaluable at the proofing stage. Photographs were reproduced from the collection preserved at the City Archives Service thanks to the co-operation of Joanne Smith. Mrs Jenie Robinson very kindly allowed us to include some examples of the work of her late father Mr Ernest Philipps, the well-known press personality. Many of the Maritime photographs contained in the book are owned by Associated British Ports and it is our pleasure to record our thanks to Laura Mark and Associated British Ports for their kind permission to reproduce them.

Thanks are also due to
Peter Thomas who penned the editorial text and
Margaret Wakefield and Andrew Mitchell for their copywriting skills.